Hjørdis Clemmensen, Viktoriia Grivina, Vasylysa Shchogoleva

Kharkiv Is a Dream
Public Art and Activism, 2013–2023

With a foreword by Bohdan Volynskyi

UKRAINIAN VOICES

Collected by Andreas Umland

73 Radomyr Mokryk
    Die ukrainischen »Sechziger«
    Chronologie einer Revolte
    ISBN 978-3-8382-1873-1

74 Leonid Finberg
    My Ukraine
    Rethinking the Past, Building the Present
    ISBN 978-3-8382-1974-5

75 Joseph Zissels
    Consider My Inmost Thoughts
    Essays, Lectures, and Interviews on Ukrainian Matters at the Turn of the Century
    ISBN 978-3-8382-1975-2

76 Margarita Yehorchenko, Iryna Berlyand, Ihor Vinokurov (eds.)
    Jewish Addresses in Ukraine
    A Guide-Book
    With a foreword by Leonid Finberg
    ISB 978-3-8382-1976-9

77 Viktoriia Grivina
    Kharkiv—A War City
    A Collection of Essays from 2022–23
    ISBN 978-3-8382-1988-2

The book series "Ukrainian Voices" publishes English- and German-language monographs, edited volumes, document collections, and anthologies of articles authored and composed by Ukrainian politicians, intellectuals, activists, officials, researchers, and diplomats. The series' aim is to introduce Western and other audiences to Ukrainian explorations, deliberations and interpretations of historic and current, domestic, and international affairs. The purpose of these books is to make non-Ukrainian readers familiar with how some prominent Ukrainians approach, view and assess their country's development and position in the world. The series was founded, and the volumes are collected by Andreas Umland, Dr. phil. (FU Berlin), Ph. D. (Cambridge), Associate Professor of Politics at the Kyiv-Mohyla Academy and an Analyst in the Stockholm Centre for Eastern European Studies at the Swedish Institute of International Affairs.

Hjørdis Clemmensen, Viktoriia Grivina,
Vasylysa Shchogoleva

KHARKIV IS A DREAM
Public Art and Activism, 2013–2023

With a foreword by Bohdan Volynskyi

Bibliografische Information der Deutschen Nationalbibliothek
Die Deutsche Nationalbibliothek verzeichnet diese Publikation in der Deutschen Nationalbibliografie; detaillierte bibliografische Daten sind im Internet über http://dnb.d-nb.de abrufbar.

Bibliographic information published by the Deutsche Nationalbibliothek
The Deutsche Nationalbibliothek lists this publication in the Deutsche Nationalbibliografie; detailed bibliographic data are available on the Internet at http://dnb.d-nb.de.

The project was supported by Documenting Ukraine, a program of the Institute for Human Sciences, IWM Vienna.

Cover design and chapter illustrations: Vasylysa Shchogoleva

Image credits:
29 / 31/ 33 Vasylysa Shchogoleva, 53 / 57 / 58 / 61 / 63 / 65 / 67 / 72 / 73 / 75 / 76 / 78 / 81 / 90 / 92 / 93 Viktoriia Grivina, 104 / 124 / 129 Hjørdis Clemmensen, 177 / 179 Viktoriia Grivina, 187 / 188 / 189 / 190 / 191 / 192 Hjørdis Clemmensen, 193 / 194 / 195 / 196 / 197 / 198 Viktoriia Grivina, 199 / 200 / 201 / 202 Vasylysa Shchogoleva

ISBN (Print): 978-3-8382-2005-5
ISBN (E-Book [PDF]): 978-3-8382-8005-9
© *ibidem*-Verlag, Hannover • Stuttgart 2025

Leuschnerstraße 40
30457 Hannover
Germany / Deutschland
info@ibidem.eu

Alle Rechte vorbehalten

Das Werk einschließlich aller seiner Teile ist urheberrechtlich geschützt. Jede Verwertung außerhalb der engen Grenzen des Urheberrechtsgesetzes ist ohne Zustimmung des Verlages unzulässig und strafbar. Dies gilt insbesondere für Vervielfältigungen, Übersetzungen, Mikroverfilmungen und elektronische Speicherformen sowie die Einspeicherung und Verarbeitung in elektronischen Systemen.

All rights reserved. No part of this publication may be reproduced, stored in or introduced into a retrieval system, or transmitted, in any form, or by any means (electronic, mechanical, photocopying, recording or otherwise) without the prior written permission of the publisher. Any person who commits any unauthorized act in relation to this publication may be liable to criminal prosecution and civil claims for damages.

Printed in the EU

Contents

Foreword by *Bohdan Volynskyi* 7

Preface 9

2023 17
    Unfiltered from the Diary 18
    When a diary goes public — street art 25

Coffee break 37
    On returning and street art 37
    Let me introduce Skovoroda 41
    All the roads lead back home 46

2018 49
    Good Conflict: The Wall of Discord and a Light Dive into Kharkiv's Aesthetics 49
    The Artist and A Window into The Grey World .. 80

Coffee break 101
    The Last Walk 101
    How I met Shevelyov 105
    Shevelovs legends 106
    On health 114
    On polyphony of voices 116
    Re: On polyphony of voices 120

2013 123
    Defining the contemporary — urban space and
    the first Ukrainian generation 124
    The chronotope; a take on time 127
    Here: yet 139

Coffee break 151
    Reflections on 2013 151
    On Shevelov and Bahtin 154
    The Fifth Kharkiv? 159

Postscript 167
    On the rebuilding of Kharkiv 167
    What comes first? 169
    Many things start with a piece of paper 181
    Dear Kharkiv 183
    Thank you notes 186

Visual Diary 188

Foreword

The image of Kharkiv was once transformed by the sounds of explosions all over the city. A big change. But not for the first time in this city. Not for the first time for the concrete highrise modernist Derzhprom building on the main square, which survived the Nazi bombing in WWII. Something remains constant. Kharkiv is on the border, and its future remains unclear. It is a city where dreamers are mixed with traders, parks with parking lots, tradition with nomadism. It is hard to explain the city, and its history is happening often without being recorded. You can read some of it in the street art on the walls, in now abandoned experimental urban developments, in the basements or hidden courtyards you can sometimes explore forming cultural institutions, 19th century buildings will show how the city's past is in dialogue with its present. If you want to understand this frontier city, you had better walk its streets. Strolling through Shevchenko's Garden full of flowers gardened by communal workers as a political tool, creating the local mayor's image, passing by people who came to take their photos in front of these flowers as a free attraction, you will eventually hear the sound of wooden decks hitting hard. It is skateboards hitting the edges to slide or jump over them in front of the brutalist opera theatre. Wooden decks are hitting this enormous and strange stone structure to shape new ways of use, to build a new tradition. You will find those skaters there even today in the third year of the full-scale russian invasion. They are skating under the air raid sirens as they were ten or 20 years ago at the same spot. Maybe it is one of the keys to understanding this city. Surely, it is better to find out more.

Bohdan Volynskyi

Preface

To those of you who don't know Kharkiv, this book will give you a glimpse of the complex and intriguing history and dynamics of the city. To those of you who are already entangled in your own love story with Kharkiv, we invite you to share your perspectives on Kharkiv with us.

Dear reader,

We are about to take you on a journey through the fabulous city of Kharkiv. This will not be a direct tour, not one of those "getting-to-know free walks" with blue umbrellas that you take on a first day in any European capital, struggling through the crowds of tourists and selfie sticks. It will be rather one of those underground dark magic kind of tours, which you start at midnight at the intersections of Whitechapel and Narnia. A trip inside the city's membrane, through its nervous system, at the end of which you might have a chance to look at your own hometown or community in a different way.

We will see how rapid the changes in the rules and laws of cohabitation can be, throw a glance at the myths and legends that hold the texture of the city together. Question philosophical backgrounds of our own knowledge-making about our homes.

We offer you three stories—three chapters—three ways to look at the city. We dig into it like archaeologists—starting with the surface layer, year 2023, gradually sinking deeper and deeper, making a stop in 2018 until we finally reach 2013. In between the three stories, we will go into stray tunnels and side-quests and view the exchange of what art, architecture, history and active communities can do to keep the city's conversations in the public space (living rooms) alive. We chose Kharkiv as an example because it is a living room that is best known to us.

But before we jump into the underground tunnel under the famous Thermometer—the ever-lively meeting spot in central Kharkiv that you can see on the cover of this volume—allow us to introduce ourselves.

The first person you will meet is Vasylysa Shchogoleva, an architect and an interdisciplinary artist living between Kharkiv and Berlin. When we think of an architect, we often imagine a calculated pragmatist whose head is filled with plans, structures and skylines. What happens when this architect sees their native city, one they used to learn to draw, in its most tragic moment, bombed and blood drained? How does an architect as a human being come to terms with the fragility of architecture, finitude of humanity and life, but also how does one hope and dream of a better city when dreams seem to be so dangerous?

The first chapter is a personal journey of an architect, a return to Kharkiv in the year of 2023 amidst the brutality of the full-scale Russian invasion. It is a diary, a confession, and an invitation to shared action and care.

The second person you will meet will be Viktoriia Grivina, a cultural anthropologist from the Kharkiv Tractor Factory district, proudly the "most dangerous district of Ukraine," according to a 2003 rating of a long-forgotten newspaper. Fascinated with street art and bickering neighbours, Viktoriia will take you to 2018, when in the very heart of the old Kharkiv centre, a small conflict between residents and artists will be seen as a promise of a better life. When the world is becoming rapidly undone, and the future in many corners of the planet becomes hazier, threatened by wars, unfreedom, and violence, can there be such a thing as a "good conflict"? Viktoriia will try to show you an example of one.

The third and final guide of this book, Hjørdis Clemmensen, a social anthropologist who had lived in Ukraine for many years, will take you all the way to the Kharkiv of 2013. Together with Hjørdis, you will arrive in a strange city on the eastern edge of Ukraine, walk from the building of the Historical Museum down the main Sumska street, and meet a group of young architects whose dreams and aspirations of Kharkiv are bold and directed towards the bright unknown of the future. Here, you will once again meet Vasylysa, now as an active participant in a group of young professionals who are not only shaping private and public space but, as Hjørdis argues, time itself. Could there be successful public activism in a country that was then becoming slowly corrupted into tyranny by the Russian-backed government of Viktor Yanukovych?

In between these stories — these highways driving you through the city — you will find an entanglement of conversations between Vasylysa, Viktoriia and Hjørdis. You will be introduced to the two thinkers who have shaped the mood, the soul, and the quirky playfulness of Kharkiv—a city of dreams. The first one—Hrihorii Skovoroda—is largely thought of as an 18th-century Ukrainian hippie, the founder of 'cardiophilosophy'— the philosophy of the heart, which fits Kharkiv like a glove. Skovoroda was both freedom-loving and serious, with a strong feel for academia, but he was also an appreciator of a good walk, good wine, cheese, and he always owned a good pair of sturdy shoes. Together with you, we will try to think about what Skovoroda and his prayer for the bright future of Kharkiv might mean. Can prophecies heal wounds? Are prophecies even real? And what does "The City of the Sun" really mean?

The second name Kharkiv is unimaginable without is George Shevelov. A historian of language and one of the brightest, shrewdest thinkers of shaping culture as an anti-colonial struggle. He is a sharp intellectual, not like the Soviet-type, docile intelligentsia, but an independent categorical idealist who preserved bits of Kharkiv's memory of the 1920s and, like a surgeon, cut the body of Kharkiv to heal it. Kharkiv is known for weapon inventions, T-34 tanks and so on, but George Shevelov might be the sharpest weapon this city has ever produced yet. His essay, "The Fourth Kharkiv," is one of the pieces the authors of this book are discussing, reading, arguing and even translating. Local myths swim around, generational differences, the influence of the Russian gaze, the sad and the hopeful.

Preface 13

This is not, as you can guess, a serious academic foliant. It is a book of snippets and dreams, written out of pure love and genuine anger, under bombings, in trains, during blackouts and missile attacks, in exile in three countries, in between many other voluntary and involuntary movements of our tired, ill, hopeful and regenerating bodies. It was written in so many states of mind. It was written during war. And so sometimes, you will find inconsistencies in writing and even views in the way we argue and change our minds. We want it to be the evidence, in a way, of what this city makes us feel. We hope you will feel something, too, reading and responding to it. We need community in these darkest times.

This book, like many other books in this world, was written during war. In the acknowledgements at the back, we will thank many people we love. Here, we want to thank our defenders, people who stand outside the city at night, listening, alert, guarding Kharkiv's sleep allowing us to be able to put words into sentences. We need community at all times, but especially in the darkest one.

The process of writing this volume also became a beacon of supportive light. In the constantly changing world, our 11.30 calls on Tuesdays and, later on, Fridays became a supportive structure in the ocean of global daily shifts as countries changed presidents and societies became more complex. This book is built on dialogue, and if during one or the other moment of reading it, you would like to share your thoughts, argument, or experience, feel free to do it via the following alleys:

Email kharkivisadream@gmail.com
Instagram @kharkivisadream
Twitter (X): @kharkivisadream
Bluesky: @kharkivisadream.bsky.social

2023

Dear Hjørdis
Dear Viktoriia

I hope you are doing well (as much as one can in these times).

As I mentioned during our last call, writing my own chapter felt for me as an intuitive process, at times as a detective one, as if I tried walking with a flashlight through the dark corners of the mind and heart. Some parts of the text were written in the moment, as diary entries, and some were written as a reflection on that. I want to stress, that life in Kharkiv is happening at a very high speed, like if you are driving a Porsche through a blaze of fire.

Therefore, the nature of this writing might be a bit chaotic, but, for me, its purpose is in documenting the city of my birth in 2023 through a personal experience. At times, I would argue with myself on the relevance of this writing, but at the same time, what keeps me doing it is a sense of – it just makes sense – along with a feeling of necessity to create a physical artefact to which I, and hopefully, others, can refer to when time would come to re-fresh the memory that quickly fades away.

Before I continue, I would also like to note, that talking about Kharkiv as a city triggers different registers in me: me as a person who was born and raised in the city, and who now lives between Kharkiv and Berlin; me as an architect, and me as an artist. What I understand is that this city is my point of strength for me and that is why I return to it again and again, and look for ways to participate in its development.

Unfiltered from the Diary

WHY

behind my trip to Ukraine in the summer of 2023

On 24.02. the reality I believed in — people will not kill other people who have different world views — crashed.

The shock of the situation mobilized me physically into the mode of volunteer — help my family, friends, and friends of friends who were fleeing in order to survive, who were remaining to protect our Home, and those who couldn't or didn't want to flee. One and a half years later I found myself on the road to my Hometown, Kharkiv, on the eastern side of Ukraine.

The last time I was here was in December 2021. Then my international friends were already alarmed by the media coverage of the troops standing at the border of my country, in close proximity to where I was. I didn't believe they would cross. I didn't believe they would shoot next to my mother's house which stands on the city's border.

Why was I going home now? I felt the need not only to see my family but also to face the New reality. A reality where physical violence was possible and is happening right now. When I was thinking about certain moments of the trip, in Berlin, I thought they would make me cry. When the moment arrived — tears didn't. I realise now that the reason for it is that the tears already happened — last year — those were the tears of grief for the reality that didn't exist anymore.

Right now I cried a few times. Once, when I walked from the bus stop towards my temporary home in Uzhhorod. Those were the tears of happiness: I have the opportunity to be on my soil.

Second, in Kharkiv, when I saw a poster about the exhibition opening of the children's artworks that happened on 21.02.2022 under the title "Almost Spring". These were the tears of loss, and the final realisation that one reality was shot and a new one needs to be constructed. But where does one start?

July 30, 2023
Kharkiv

When during the first night I heard explosions for the first time I unconsciously moved my pillow from under the window to the door. Thinking — at least like this I may save my head from the broken glass in case of the explosion wave. Nothing would save me in case of a direct hit.

My body got cold that moment as I was thinking of it. I put on my blue & yellow hoodie, socks and managed to fall asleep for a while before the next air raid alarm hit my ears.

August 6, 2023
Kharkiv

I went to see my grandparents. Doing manual labour freed some part of me, so that when I came back to Kharkiv, — words, images, ideas, — started to pour through me.

Maybe one needs to come to the starting point for the new reality to get loaded through the action and time. But what to do with the threat to physical existence as an air alarm keeps crushing the cityscape during the day and night? Does the new reality contain acceptance of finite existence at any given moment?

I keep thinking — everything has a price. My life can be one of them.

This is what New Reality has to offer, yet, again.

My calendar entry mentions: August 11, 2023, 16.00 Meeting Tanya Pukhnavtseva. Tanya is a fellow artist and we haven't seen each other for ages. It is funny, how meeting people in Kharkiv these days became something of a special treat. Many of us are now all over the world: different cities, and different countries, but once we see on social media geolocation — Kharkiv — we click our messengers and arrange a meeting, as if seeing each other would help us go through this chapter by connecting the dots between our past, present and, hopefully, future life's. During these meetings we often update each other on what has happened to us since 24.02.2022. Did we believe in the potential full-scale invasion? How did we react when it actually happened? How long did we remain in the city? (Those of us, like me, who don't — how long did it take us to finally be able to arrive in the city).

August 11, 2023
Kharkiv

We meet Tanya and her friend, Viktoriia (whom you will meet in the next chapter of this book). She wants both of us to meet, as we are all passionate about Kharkiv. We will meet at the bottom of the city, and then we want to walk past one of my *love-medicine interventions (plasters) to check if it is still there. The moment we arrive at it, Viktoriia takes pictures and asks me to tell the story of how it happened that I put this work here. So I start:*

I was walking in the city; it was a very hot day, and I had few 'love-medicine' plasters left. I was walking up the street, just like us now, and I noticed a guy taking a photo of the woman from across the street. I stopped to observe. The woman was trying to cover something on this piece of the wall with a spray can. The guy was upset about her action. The word in question was "occupant." I told him that it was best to come and ask her why she was doing it before jumping to conclusions. So I crossed the street and asked her:

- *Why are you covering this word?*
- *My boss called me (she has been abroad since the invasion) and asked me to cover it because our clients are asking her, why is "occupant" written on our shop?*
- *You know, I have this plaster with me; should we see if it covers the word?*
- *Oh, really? How much would it cost?*
- *Oh, I didn't plan for it. In case you want to pay, maybe, you could cover the material costs? But also, I just want to help you.*

We try it out, and the plaster fits. The woman is happy and really wants to thank me back for my work and invites me for a coffee — we agree it would be the best way to conclude this exchange. We decide to take a walk up the street, as she needs to go to a pharmacy, and I need to go in the same direction to get some more art supplies. In the end, we spend a long part of the day together; I show her the city, and she tells me her story. As the conversation keeps flowing, we return back to the shop. She invites me inside and offers me to select anything I like. It is an antique shop, and there are many beautiful items. I chose a tiny blue vase, and she complemented it with a yellow one. As I turn them up-side down, I see the manufacturing country — Germany — I smile, as I think about how I will take these two items back to where they were made in my bag.

I realised in that moment that my job here is not just to make but also to listen.

Now, we are walking the same street and continue the conversation with Tanya and Viktoriia. We arrive at a cosy Kharkiv space — Coffee Makers. Tanya's studio is nearby, and I am excited to see what she is working on, so we decided to go there — the mecca of Kharkiv art studios — where many Kharkiv artists started their path. Coincidentally, it is on the same street as the studio where Hjørdis was recording her interviews, and where the architectural community grew, turning the space into a common studio, workshop and lecture hall (you will meet Hjørdis and visit the studio in Chapter Three).

August 12, 2023
Kharkiv

It's raining today. I have only three days left in Kharkiv. This makes me sad. For the first time during my stay here I felt sad when I was walking the half-empty park. This was the moment I felt the pain of the war. Many people still haven't returned here. The space feels extra vast. At the same time, I remind myself that this is the spirit of Kharkiv, founded on the steppe as a fortress. This is exactly what makes this place — its raw *essence that creates circumstances in which you experience life in its purest form.*

I felt sad also because I was scared to leave Kharkiv. I am scared that I might be naive, as in December 2021. Then, I also felt happy and hopeful about the growing opportunity for building a bridge between Kharkiv and Berlin, Kharkiv and the rest of the world. After these days, I am hopeful again. I might be naive, but I know how to face the darkest chapters and come out the other side, again.

Kharkiv is wounded, but alive.
So am I.

August 17, 2023
Lviv

I am sitting on the sofa under the window in the new home of my Kharkiv friend and former Red Cross colleague, Lika. I am filling out a Google form. It's an Open Call under the title "Care" organised by my friend Anna. I quickly type, as I don't have much time, but I feel that I must tell the world that Kharkiv is alive:

Last week, I came to my native Kharkiv for the first time since the 24th of February 2022. The last time I was in the city was in December 2021 with an urban project in Saltivka. We wanted to continue, but the war put everything on pause.

So when last week I met an energetic guy named Magran, who, together with friends and colleagues, created a pop-up exhibition in the city in April 2023 and asked me to hold a workshop in their space, I immediately agreed. This is a story about the creative life of Kharkiv, which is in full swing every day. To understand what Kharkiv is like now, imagine plywood with the inscription "We're open." The desire to live life here and now is the driving force. Being in the same city at the same time allowed this initiative to happen so spontaneously. After this accidental meeting, we concluded that we want to continue developing such workshops in Kharkiv. We are currently thinking about finding grants for support.

February 1–6, 2025
Berlin

For the past few weeks, I have been going back and forth between timelines in my own head during the day, but also during the night. Last week, I had more dreams than usual. I noticed that it happened to me also after my previous returns from Kharkiv. From time to time, I dream about war. This time, the dream was something from… I am scared to keep typing this, as if it's some kind of prediction, and I wish this timeline would not unfold.

 I guess it's true what we discussed with Viktoriia in her residency's kitchen: during a time of change, people might go closer to the spiritual, beyond logic, to process and understand things from a new perspective. But, it feels like something to be contemplated in the next book and here I need to wrap up my chapter.

 I think, or rather, I feel, that **once I accepted the reality, I could go back to a certain normality, where I took a piece of paper in my hands and started making.** *For* me, *art is the light that helped me to cross to the other side and keep walking. Just like in the song:*

> "...we have two walls: love & labor,
> and maybe exactly they make us."
> (Misha Pravylnyi)

As I am reviewing this writing at the Admiralbrücke on the 7th of March 2025 under the rays of sun, surrounded by people who are discussing the current political situation in Spanish, English, German and other tongues, I note on the draft of the manuscript: *my motivation behind writing this chapter, as in my work in general, is to inspire others to take matters in their own hands, even, if, at first, things seem blurry, or not to make sense, but a sentence a day might lead you to a chapter in a book and a book might brings you to a next place and that is how one can actively co-create new worlds where power is not about violence, but about strength to withstand strong winds and blossom with new fresh leaves of Hope.*

On that note, I want to finish this chapter with the two artworks I did during my stay in Kharkiv in the summer of 2023:

When a diary goes public — street art

To heal

To heal is a multi-part urbanistic intervention that I realised in my hometown, Kharkiv, with the desire to heal the wounds caused by russian aggression. You already read about one of the works earlier when we walked with Tanya and Viktoriia. Below is the story of the second out of four plasters in the urban space of Kharkiv, told in a mix of my artistic and architectural voices, as some parts of the text come from my portfolio.

Coming and going to Kharkiv became part of me in the autumn of 2015, or, maybe, even earlier. I often came up with a mission, purpose or project. This time, on my way home, I started to invent a task for myself.

Once I arrived in Kharkiv I went to the art supply shop I have known for a long time. Encountering items in the same places as before 24.02.2022 felt comforting. The same goes for the shop owner with whom we had a chat about the durability of the supplies I was buying for my street interventions.

July 2023: I chose a corner of Constitution Square, as, at the time, it felt like the heart of the city for me. This corner suffered a missile attack that caused a huge wound. I remember seeing images and videos from that day on my phone back in my Berlin flat. I remember crying. So when I was on the bus and thinking about my potential artwork for the city, this place came to my mind, and the idea for a plaster was born, as I felt that, as an architect, I might not be able to cure this place right now, but as a human, I felt that I want to do something right now, even if it was simply placing a curing symbol. In this way, I wanted to show my love for my hometown and somehow, while doing it—thinking about Kharkiv, thinking about ideas of various artistic gifts for it, and then, actually, cutting the cardboard, the foil and gluing it on the corner, I felt, that **it's not that I healed the city, but it healed me.**

August 2023: Graffiti was placed next to the plaster on Constitution Square by an unknown person. It contained two articles of the constitution referring to the medical rights of citizens. I found it funny and exciting at the same time. The architect inside me thought — wow! This person co-created and marked this space, which means he/she feels he/she has the same right to the city as me. It felt important for me to note this, as this type of interaction was not the case in my earlier city experiences.

Autumn 2023: After a few months, I got a photo from my father, where I could see that the work, along with the graffiti, had been covered with a layer of yellow paint. Once I zoomed in on the photo, I could see that someone tried to remove the work, but wasn't successful. The "Tritonchyk" glue from Severodonetsk proved to be stronger (*thanks to the advice of the shop owner*).

I don't know, who exactly, covered the work, but my guess, is it was communal workers. I could understand this act as a way of calming the buzz at this highly controversial corner of public space, as I noticed during my intervention there, that other controversial writings on the wall were appearing here, that might not be on the time for a discussion at the front-line city, where environment is heated enough already. Therefore, I wasn't upset, in the end, the beauty of street art is in it's temporality.

January 2024: I presented the photo of the work and corner in question, during the group exhibition POLY:LUX in Berlin-Kreuzberg. The photo was placed in the window, creating a visual connection between Kharkiv's and Berlin's urban spaces.

February 2024: during my visit to Kharkiv, I printed the photo of the Berlin's window, with the 'lovemedicne' work from the Kharkiv's corner, on a set of A4 papers and placed it on top of the yellow paint, while adding a description about the work and a QR-code to my Instagram page, in case, someone would like to get in touch with me. So far, no one has. At this time, the corner was surrounded by a structure that resembled a fence. It was made out of wood. I am guessing, the purpose of it was to protect passers-bys from the potential harm that could be caused due to the ruination of the building. Let's see what happens next; maybe it is a new window of opportunities?

Later on, in my artistic portfolio, I would write: "Such interactions are one of the forms of dialogue I pursue in public space, offering, building, and consolidating low-threshold bridges of exchange."

December 2024: the window is now covered with a large banner print, as the nearby corner has been decorated for the Christmas holidays. The wooden fence has been exchanged for a metal mesh on which a street exhibition of children's artworks is being displayed.

I am happy to see how this corner transformed itself into a gallery. The process of it's realisation and aesthetics I will leave for another conversation.

Riders

Driving to Kharkiv felt like a spiritual experience for me this time. Going home for the first time since it withstood a storm of missiles felt differently. I am not sure I can put it well into words, but I will try. When on the first day of my stay, I got a chance to walk on the streets of my city, I stumbled into a courtyard and saw a poster for a children's art exhibition from 21.02.2022. Tears rolled down my cheeks. Tears of loss over the reality that was shot. A new one needs to be constructed. But where to start?

Producing art for my city felt meaningful. I chose a subject that, as I felt then, was familiar to many of us — a long bus journey. At the same time, I felt that it was a process that we experienced before the invasion too, and, therefore, it felt like an invisible connection to civilian life, where joy and happiness of the bus ride to a new place, or as now, to a family, would connect the dots between now and then, creating a space for tomorrow.

I had some of the cardboard left from the 'love-medicine' plasters (to heal), and I had already tested how to

mount it on the street, so I decided to stick to this material as a base for the painting. My father's balcony became my improvised studio for this visit. It was perfect — I could see the city in front of me, and I could place long pieces of cardboard on the floor. Working on this piece, same as typing about it, was an intuitive process and, at times, unclear, but, somehow, I kept doing it, as I felt it made sense to me. As my stay in Kharkiv was coming to an end, I needed to choose the location for my work. At this point, my father and I shared numerous conversations about my work, the city and life. So when I said it was time to mount the work, we came to a common conclusion, that this time, it would be good to place it in such a way that it was a bit higher than a person's height. For that, I would need a ladder, and my dad, had one in his office.

Of course, I could write some more artistically or architecturally sophisticated reasons, but you know, war has shown me that the motivation behind my work has always been about joy, about making people smile, feel seen and feel like they too can do things, and can participate in the creation of the space around them.

At the same time, you remember, as a child, to whom did you gift your first drawings? Probably, your loved ones. So, when things collapsed altogether, I felt it was meaningful to make a gift to my family and friends and, maybe, through that, those to whom it would speak. On the day when we were mounting the work with my father, passers-by were stopping for a chat. The glue behind the cardboard somehow, didn't want to work on that hot summer day, so my father's colleague gave us nails and a hammer. I felt happy. I felt closer to architecture — I was finally hammering nails into a wall. I felt as if the shadow of the war allowed the sun to come out behind the clouds for a moment. I remember, almost, every talk I had that day.

I remember two Anjas — one from Kharkiv and one from Jena (Germany) — photography students who stopped to take a photo of us. It's not possible to plan for such an occasion; it was a pure thing of the moment. I remember my father and I smiling while posing for a photo. At that moment, the next idea came to my mind. As I posted on social media about the work, I couldn't quite find the words to explain what I had just done, so

I typed, "Kharkiv is a dream", triptych, acrylics on cardboard, 33.3 x 210 cm, Kharkiv, 2023. The next day, I cut out the letters of the title in English and Ukrainian, and nailed them onto the sides of the work.

Later, an artist friend, told me about his professor, who said that an artist's life is a performance. Well, this performance is unfolding in front of me each day. However, I wish, the price for it would not be this high. It's hard for me to type these words here because I am scared. Scared of judgement, scared of hurting someone else's feelings, being inconsiderate, not inclusive and so forth. At the same time, I want to tell you this story the way I got to experience it, simply, because I can type it in English, so that you, my foreign friend, might feel me, and, hopefully, would want to go to Kharkiv and take a photo next to the bus riders, as my friends, who are in Kharkiv, or who visit it have been doing for the past years.

That's another story to be told. For now, I leave you with a QR code to a video that ties together some of the stories you read here, as I read them out loud during the group exhibition in Berlin, while bringing the copy of the bus riders to the Berlin space, as a bridge to Kharkiv's street and my, personal dream, of people and places to be interconnected for common support and resilience. Enjoy the ride and see you, in Kharkiv.

Coffee break

On returning and street art

From Viktoriia

Hi, Vasylysa,
I just wanted to say that I felt something very similar on my first return to Kharkiv. I like how you write, "as I walked my city," because my first thoughts — it was June 2022 — were similar. I thought, "What have they done to MY city?" And then, this immediate desire to create something kicks in. You want to cover all the walls with new layers of paint, and put all the windows back, and get into the archives, and look how we can restore these beautiful historical buildings, and why some don't have the right status, take better care of everything. And then you just want to do something with your hands. I brought books for recycling on that first summer, their weight, the lightness I felt after, was liberating. I really admire your approach as a street artist. As Jaime Lerner put it, acupuncture of the city is your ability to bring healing via art. Street art might be temporary in form, but it can leave deep cultural and social reflection. And I think for this woman you helped, for her, street art has become visible, maybe for the first time in her life, and thanks to you in a good way.

Anyhow, I have been thinking how interlinked the stories are, of today's Kharkiv public art, how we treat our shared city, and how we need to understand that we share it with very different people. It should be a conversation, not a monologue, as you've smartly noted recently. The processes of re-

viewing this shared space that started in the 1990s, continue to this day, war or no war. Today we have the culmination of a certain interesting journey of a Kharkivian, from a Soviet citizen who lived in the city where nothing was permitted, to this liberal city where many things are permitted, but also where you are directly responsible for how your street looks. It's a tremendous journey. Now, perhaps, this habit has become strong enough for us to think, "nah, Russia won't tell us how our city will look like. Never again." It's up to us what to paint. Also, funnily, what not to paint.

Viktoriia

On leaving in Feb '22 and visiting Lviv

Dear Vasylysa and Viktoriia
It is such a valuable gift to be able to start working from a blank sheet of paper — to have a tool that can help you process this confusing time. We are thankful that you share your works with us and the city.

My tools are anthropological methods — observing, talking to people, and writing down what I see, hear, and how I feel. My brain is spinning from trying to analyse what's going on now. It has been difficult at best but impossible most of the time.

Your reflections from your first visit to Kharkiv evoked a lot of emotions and memories for me. I'd like to share a few reflections from my own experience of leaving Ukraine right before the war and finding my way back to the new Ukraine.

You mentioned the poster saying "almost spring." It speaks directly to the feelings of loss and grief that seem to have moved in with me permanently. I don't want to linger with those emotions but let me just briefly tell you how we left and what happened next. I had just moved in with my boyfriend and his son in Kyiv in the autumn of 2021 in a home we had bought together. We decorated the place with plants and put up shelves. We were getting to know the neighbours. We had an extra bedroom for a future second child. In February 2022 we understood that it would be good to spend a few weeks in Lviv until the tension on the border blew over. I haven't been back to Kyiv since. Our home is still there, our things are still there, our plants are still there, thriving under the care of a friend who has already experienced spring three times in our home. I did not get to spend a single one there.

You went back to Kharkiv in the summer of 2023, partly to face the new reality. Like with Kyiv, I have not made it back to Kharkiv yet, even though I have called it my home in the past. It turned out that I was pregnant when we left Ukraine. I had a son in November 2022. Life kept happening in the most tangible of ways. Now in Vienna. I have not wanted to leave my son for more than a few days and I have not wanted to bring him with me to Ukraine either. Not yet.

I did finally go to Lviv in the spring of 2024. Just setting my feet on Ukrainian soil and breathing the air made a huge difference to me. The smells. The sounds. Rattling trams. The reflection of the sun in the guitar held by a woman performing next to the Shevchenko Monument. The taste of fries and milk stout in a pub. The jittery feeling of having too many fancy coffees in one morning. The feeling of being under-dressed for the stylish, urban culture… big, quiet parks with benches and lamps of twirling metal. Merch with the message, "Be brave like Ukrainians." Well, that one was new. Air raids. Also new.

While I was in Lviv I dropped by the Kharkiv School of Architecture that had relocated there as a consequence of the full-scale invasion. The second-year students were showing their works, offering their ideas for a housing project for internally displaced persons. They had come up with creative solutions that were culturally meaningful, environmentally sustainable, and cleverly designed for people with disabilities. There were lots of awesome ideas that filled me with inspiration and hope for a flourishing future, once the war was over. During a break I chatted to one of the students. I asked her if she had relocated to Lviv when the school moved. "Yes," she replied, "I relocated to Lviv to continue my studies. My grandmother refuses to be evacuated from her village north of Kharkiv. I have lost my brother in the war." She paused, "I have a hard time focusing on this project." I turned away, suddenly distracted by something unimportant. It took me several minutes for her words to get through to me. When I finally did allow myself to hear her, she had turned away and was speaking to other people. I quietly murmured, "I am so sorry."

Nothing was the same. The war was not over. I had to let go of the Ukraine I knew, the peaceful Ukraine packed with dreams and aspirations, where every new day revealed yet more proof that this country is headed somewhere awesome. I had to face the new reality. Ukraine is at war, fighting for a future.

I guess I am slowly resurfacing, now as a less naive version of myself. I no longer take peace and freedom for granted. Invasions happen; it is not a concept of the past, as I used to believe. People are tortured and killed. Territorial integrity is not a thing if you cannot defend your territory. With the political developments in the US and the imperialistic visions they exhibit it is better to understand sooner rather than later that we live in a world where physical violence, as you put it, is a legitimate way of getting what you want. There are no global rules that guarantee human rights and there is no global police out there to enforce anything or protect anyone. I see this now, and I appreciate the clarity.

I find myself as a schizophrenic European (now a Danish refugee from Ukraine, based in Vienna), who understands Ukraine very well. For so many years Ukraine seemed very far away to most people in Western Europe. Not anymore. It is clear to everyone that we are closely connected, but it worries me that people here in Western Europe still seem to take freedom for granted and still seem to think that everything will be good if we just all live according to positive values, talk about our differences, and exchange goods with each other. I hope that we can mobilise, act, and fight like the Ukrainians have done.

My visit to Lviv and working on this book with you are helping me adjust to the new reality, little by little. It is healing. Thank you.

Hjørdis

Let me introduce Skovoroda

From Viktoriia

Hi, Hjørdis
There is a philosopher from the 1700's Kharkiv called Skovoroda. He might say that working on this book is "related

work," something we do because it feels right. Skovoroda was a pretty chill guy who liked to walk in nature outside of Kharkiv with his walking stick.

Skovoroda legends

(in the flawed words of Viktoriia Grivina)

> *Де багато любові, там багато помилок.*
> *Де немає любові, там все — помилка.*
> *Бери вершину і матимеш середину.*
>
> *Where there is love, there are many mistakes.*
> *Where there is no love — everything is a mistake.*
> *Strive for the top and you'll get a middle.*
> H. Skovoroda

In the 1920s, a group of ethnographers from Kharkiv travelled to the Babaii area of Kharkiv region to record local people's tales and legends. In the course of interviews they couldn't help asking villagers about Hryhorii Skovoroda, a wandering philosopher who lived in the region for a long time. "Sure, we know Hryhorii Savvych," one peasant woman said, "We've seen him many times." The ethnographers gave her a puzzled look, "You mean, your ancestors talked to Skovoroda?" "Why ancestors? I talked to him myself a couple of years ago," the woman answered earnestly. She wasn't the only one who told this story. The stunned ethnographers returned to Kharkiv thinking about all those people who told them of hanging out with the 18th-century wandering philosopher as if he was their best buddy. How relative is time? How close some people are, stretching their hand across centuries to the lands that remember them so vividly.

The legend of Hryhorii Skovoroda is that of happiness. His 'cardiophilosophy' — philosophy of the heart — said that life is about searching for happiness. Ukrainian cardiophilosophical legend says one day, a Russian empress, Catherine II, was travelling through Sloboda, Ukraine and met Skovoroda as he walked with his famous stick across the field. She ordered to bring the philosopher to her and told him to come with her to St Petersburg, where gold and riches awaited him (alongside St Petersburg's torture chambers, of course, which always come with the deal). Skovoroda smiled politely and said, "I won't leave Ukraine. A pipe and a sheep are worth more than a tsar's crown to me" [Для мене дудка та вівця дорожче царського вінця]. Skovoroda said that there are three worlds and two natures. Three worlds included a macrocosm, all the living world, a microcosm, the world of a human, and the Bible/God. All of that had two natures, a visible nature — a world of things — and an invisible nature — the essence and the soul of things. Apparently, Catherine II could offer none of that to the philosopher.

Skovoroda also had two modes of existence, depending on the season. In the summer and warm weather months, he walked across Sloboda Ukraine, talked to people, chilled. Did a lot of cardio. During winters and cold months, he would settle in one of his friends' mansions and write, putting in the form of philosophical conversations and fables all the wisdom he received during his summer fieldwork.

Skovoroda was a vegetarian, stepping carefully on the ground so as not to hurt a single living thing. He ate once or twice a day, but really loved good Parmeggiano cheese and red Hungarian wines. He had a fancy watch and good shoes. Otherwise, had no earthly possessions.

Skovoroda's main ideas were that of harmonious/related work, unequal equality, and a philosophical fountain of wisdom. He said people should do what harmonises with their inclinations, work at the job they love, to put it simply, everyone is equal but has different levels of talent and should be rewarded according to their talents. And all of us need to strive to drink from the fountain of wisdom. Fountain fills jugs of different capacities and forms; thus, life gives everyone according to their needs and potentials. You can see that fountain on a 500-hundred hryvnia banknote.

When Skovoroda came to Kharkiv to teach at a local collegium (a precursor of Kharkiv University), the city was very small and could be almost entirely fitted on an island between two rivers, Lopan and Kharkiv. Skovoroda settled behind the river Kharkiv, an area of orchards and windmills that was then called "Zakharkiv" ["Behind Kharkiv River"]. For that reason, Skovoroda called Kharkiv the city of the prophet Zakharia [Zechariah], the Memory of God, i.e. one who God remembers, the city of the Future and the city of the Sun. Skovoroda's 1790 prayer for Kharkiv," Oratio ad deum in urbem Zacharpolim," goes,

> Zechariah says, you have seven eyes.
> The seventh eye is the city of Zechariah
> To these seven eyes only you, Christ, is the pupil,
> Blind are the eyes when the pupil is closed,
> Oh, open your eyes, look at it!
> Thus the city of Zechariah will become the real sun![1]

Given that Zechariah was one of the scariest eschatological prophets, predicting the end of the world and such, having him on our side would be a reassuring development. But also, it is interesting how Skovoroda hints at Campanella here, weaving philosophy and theology together. His messages are always more complicated than you think.

The 18th century, the time when Skovoroda lived, was called "the century of defeat for Ukraine" — as contemporary philosopher Oleksandr Filonenko notes.[2] And yet, it gave birth to the most optimistic Ukrainian philosopher ever. His philosophy is baroque in its style,

---

1   Захарія прорікає, що в тебе сім очей.
    Сьоме око — місто Захарія.
    Цим семи очам ти єдиний, Христе, зіниця.
    Сліпі очі, коли закрита зіниця.
    О розкрий свої очі, зглянься на нього!
    Так місто Захарія буде справжнім сонцем.
2   "У чому феномен Сковороди та як він допоміг пережити полон: Козловський, Лютий та Філоненко про Григорія Сковороду" Suspilne Kultura, 3 December 2023.

but individualistic. It reverberates with Spinosa's monism and, at the same time, the mystical aspect of Kierkegaard. It is, like his walks, a very chaotic scripture intermingled with a good deal of humour, and, very ironically for a city of the universities, sciences and so on, Skovoroda makes Kharkiv the centre of the philosophy of the heart. Think with your heart, he says, poking the lazy Kharkiv soil with his famous walking stick.

[ADD LINKS TO **SERIOUS** SCIENTIFIC ARTICLES ABOUT SKOVORODA][3]

All the roads lead back home

Dear Viktoriia,

Thank you very much for introducing Skovoroda on these pages. I remember, that summer day of 2023, when I stumbled upon a mural portraying him and his wisdom to us on the

---

3 We decided to leave this screaming line as a reminder of our passionate conversations over this book. But if you came here for an honest advice, here it is.
The best text to start with is Skovoroda's biography by Leonid Ushkalov. Ushkalov undertook a tremendous job not only having created an impressive body or research, but promoting memory of Skovoroda across the region.
Ushkalov, Leonid, Catching an Elusive Bird: The Life of Hryhorii Skovoroda / Leonid Ushkalov ; Translated from the Ukrainian by Natalia Komarova., trans. by Natalia Komarova (ibidem-Verlag, 2024).
For all familiar with Ukrainian, Taras Lyutyi is a contemporary philosopher who gives a fresh reading of Skovoroda's legacy, Лютий, Тарас, Сковорода. Самовладання, (Темпора, 2022).

corner covered with OSB boards, as the windows were crushed by a missile:

"Be like a palm tree: The tighter the rock squeezes it, the faster and more beautifully it rises upward." [Уподібнюйся пальмі: Чим міцніше її стискає скеля, тим швидше і прекрасніше здіймається вона догори.]

I don't know who put them there, but I am grateful for it, as these words felt to me, in that moment, as the best words of a warm support and reassurance that I need to keep going, keep cutting my plasters, paint paintings, talk to people and, simply, be.

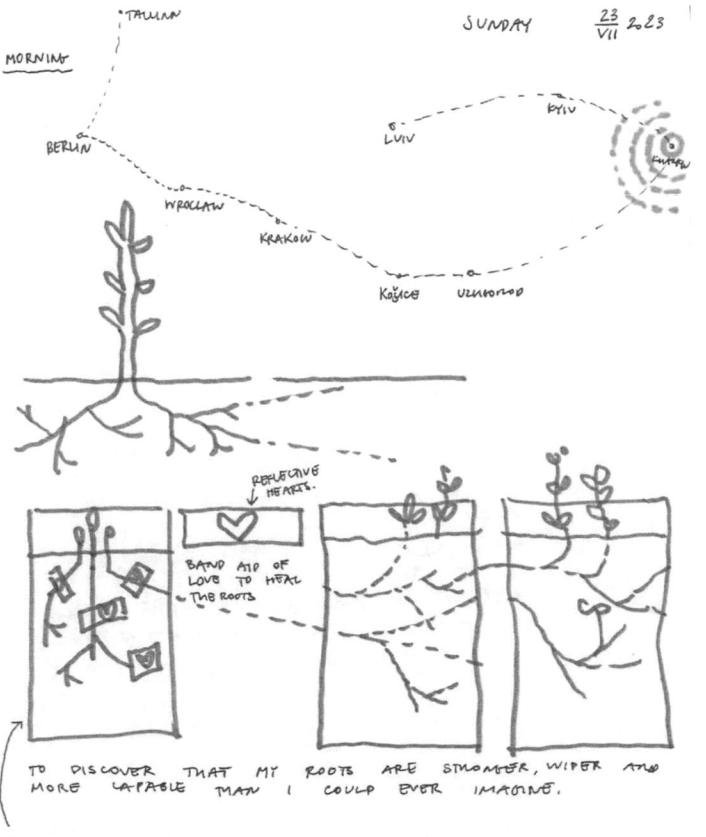

2018

Dear Vasylysa and Hjørdis,
Going further back, I think this story might be relevant to our discussion on public community and art. It is a story I explored back in 2018 for my master's dissertation, and I often return to it when thinking of the possible futures of Kharkiv.

Good Conflict: The Wall of Discord and a Light Dive into Kharkiv's Aesthetics

Introduction

> *In 2018, an artwork created on an electric booth by a local artist, Hamlet Zinkivskiy, was painted over by the neighbours. A scandal erupted – did these people have the right to cover uncommissioned art? Social, political, or humorous writings started to appear on the freshly painted wall every night. Every day, municipal workers would cover it all with a thick layer of grey paint. The conflict led to the great re-negotiation of unspoken rights and rules of art production and tolerance in the city. The Wall became a legend, a myth, a style. In short, a Kharkiv Dream.*

In the past decade, I've spent approximately four years travelling, volunteering, working, or studying "in Europe", i.e. away from Kharkiv.[4] On every return, I had

---

4   For many years, I tried to prove to Ukrainians and the world that Ukraine was part of Europe. I don't do it now, as I don't feel European at the moment. But do any Europeans feel European? During a recent flight from Edinburgh to Frankfurt, a border officer asked me, "When did you arrive in Europe?" "I've literally never been outside of it", I wanted to answer and held myself, in fear I would be refused entry "to Europe". What the officer wanted to know was when I'd left the UK, a country swiftly expelled from Europe in the popular imagination of the

to reintroduce myself to the city, like one gets re-acquainted with a cat that forgets about your existence the minute you go out of the door. Every time, changes revealed themselves in us both. The story I am about to tell happened in the early autumn of 2018. About to set off on an Erasmus Mundus Master's programme, I was in Kharkiv, working on a project that documented stories of internally displaced persons from Donbas.[5] Running from one interview to another, I didn't have time to take part in the Wall of Discord. The story had such resonance, however, that it reached my ears unwittingly through the evening talks with art curators in the kitchens or in the social media posts I read while running across Freedom Square to work in debates and discussions we had with international volunteers during lunch breaks. In short, it came in the most urban way possible — through natural immersion into Kharkiv city space. It finally got under my skin so deep I had to write

---

"continentals". But the question lingered. Had I ever been to Europe? Did it even exist? If it did, I was probably not invited. When another border officer sorted lines at passport control in Stuttgart, shouting "European/Non-European", I obediently stood in the latter line with my fellow Syrians and Taiwanese. On a deeply philosophical level, European airports have been a fantastic field for autoethnographic observations. But I only ever felt welcome flying to the Kharkiv airport, the magical place where Ukrainian passport was a pro rather than a con.

5   In my then uneducated mind, Donbas wasn't yet a problematic term. Only now it comes so clearly as an exploitative concept, valuable by the former Russian (and some other) empires only for its resources — "Donetsk coal basin".

an Erasmus Mundus Master's dissertation about the Wall to get it out of my system.[6]

Growing up on the fringes of a big city, I've always been fascinated with margins, borders, and transgressions, things that happen out of the corner of your eye. Footnotes in the books, Derrida argued, can overpower the main text. He called this phenomenon parergon.[7] And this chapter is really a parergon to my Master's Dissertation with its overly highbrow title, "Street Art and Community Development in Kharkiv, Ukraine." The story came from the margins — city rumours, long walks around Kharkiv, attempts to document and understand its aesthetics, chasing down and interviewing interesting Kharkivians in myths and legends, and gods the citizens of this unimaginable megapolis were praying to in 2018. About 90% of the talks with the said interesting Kharkivians did not make it into the dissertation. Righting the wrongs, I will try to deepen the aesthetic unconsciousness of Kharkiv[8], the traits that the Wall highlighted, and the stories it concealed.

---

6   You can, at your own risk, read this dissertation, "The Influence of Street Art on Community Development in Kharkiv, Ukraine" by accessing its (forgive me for it) page on Academia https://www.academia.edu/44879456/Masters_Dissertation_The_Influence_of_Street_Art_on_Community_Development_in_Kharkiv_Ukraine
7   Derrida, Jacques, and Craig Owens. "The parergon." October 9 (1979): p.3-41.
8   Isn't it fun to make up terms? By "aesthetic unconsciousness" I simply mean the aesthetics of Kharkiv streets, a certain set of unspoken style preferences locals chose when they look around

An anecdotal story set against the fourth year of the Russian war in Ukraine, in a fragile nook between 2014 and 2022, will open the door to a fundamental question: where does our home end? At the apartment entrance door, a little garden outside, or a pavement around, or every building along our street? For street art, home is the whole city. This chapter is about the ability to dream of Kharkiv through street art.

The Wall of Discord

Early autumn in Kharkiv is a lovely time. The drastic heat of the steppe gives way to moderate warmth and violet evenings, and the entire city is buzzing with students returning from summer break. The smell of freshly printed books is mixed with the burnt leaves of the first autumn fires, illegal and secretly encouraged by communal workers. The evenings are filled with guitar playing in the residential courtyards, the first college parties, theatres' premieres, and loud street races along Science Avenue fill the air. By all accounts, a blessed time.

On one of such lovely evenings in early September 2018, equally distant from the two world-shattering winters of 2014 and 2022, a group of local art connoisseurs were passing by Gogol Street when they saw an equally notable group of people painting a wall. At first

---

to and to fit their public spaces — cafes/facades/even style in clothes — to harmonize with the existing city aesthetics. Where does this aesthetics come from though? A good question.

glance, there was nothing strange about it. Street artists in Kharkiv, like in many cities across the world, were balancing between the good and the strict side of local police, and darkness often provided the peace and quiet needed for their creativity. Having approached the painters, however, passers-by were surprised to see that rather than creating art, the people were covering a piece of art (Fig 1) with a thick, monotonous layer of grey paint.

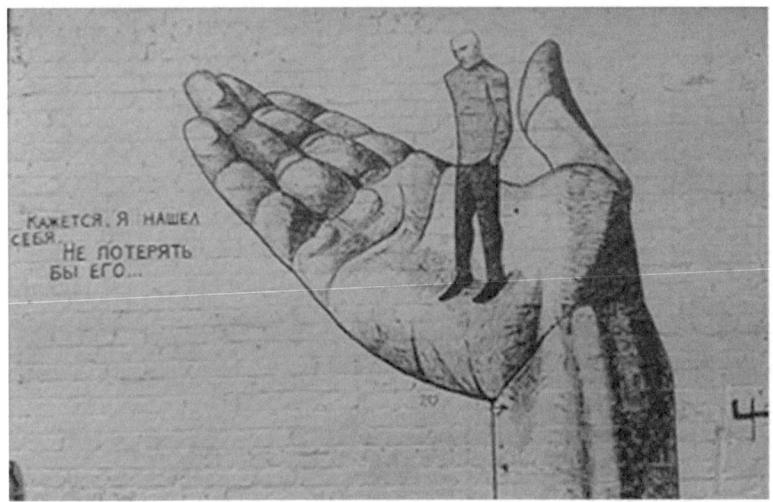

Fig. 1. "I think I've found myself, hope not to lose him," — original work by Hamlet Zinkivskiy

[7th Rule
The artwork itself was created in 2016 by Hamlet Zinkivskyi and was part of the project "7-e Pravilo" (The Seventh Rule). A caption to an image of a figure standing on one's open hand said, *"I think I have found myself. Hope not to lose him."* The project was inspired by a Ukrainian writer, Taras Pro-

hasko, who had drafted six rules of life and offered his readers to find the seventh on their own.[9] Following Prohasko's suit, Hamlet made a new sketch every day for a year, creating 365 new rules. Some rules were reproduced on Kharkiv walls. The work existed for nearly two years, which in the frames of street art is a long time. Talking about all the richness of responses to the destruction of the mural, the mural itself gets somehow lost, yet it is precisely the work that ignited, disturbed and motivated the paint over. What was it about the mural that stirred a local household?]

The people who decided to paint over Zinkivskyi's 7th Rule were a family whose kitchen windows overlooked the wall and who had grown so unhappy with their view they decided to take matters into their own hands.

"It's schizophrenia," the mother and spokesperson of the family replied when asked what they thought was wrong with the artwork. Attempts to convince the family that it was a valuable piece did not have much effect; the painting was quickly covered, and the satisfied family returned to their apartment, convinced that the issue was resolved.

Far from it, the act of painting over the wall stirred something deeply fundamental in the balance of Kharkiv's public life. The chain of events that followed became known as the Wall of Discord, or, more precisely, "The Wall of Sratch."[10] Having taken place on

---

9   Nastya Kalyta, 'Gamlet: pro graffiti, junist ta ukrainsku movu' ('Hamlet: On Graffiti, Youth and Ukrainian language'), Your Art, July, 10, 2019.
10 Originated from a colloquial expression that can be vaguely translated as "to shit' (sratj)", the word "srach" has become a popular denominator of heated arguments, especially on social

Gogol Street, the conflict had nothing to do with the most ambiguous of all Ukrainian writers, Mykola, aka Nikolai Gogol; the mural of Gogol's characters by Hamlet Zinkivskyi and Roman Minin metres away remained untouched, despite its close proximity to the Cathedral of the Assumption of the Blessed Virgin Mary[11] Neither did the scandal touch the nearby bust of a Russian imperial poet, Aleksandr Pushkin, with its chipped head, the reminder of the Mykola Mikhnovsky.[12]

The conflict had seemingly nothing to do with politics at all. On the surface, it was just about a family of local homeowners who had a ladder, a good amount of grey paint, and an unstoppable desire to cover a mural on an electric booth that was overlooking their windows. Jacques Rancière would argue that it was exactly the most political situation ever — city dwellers intrude into the public space, making it more comfortable and aesthetically pleasing for them.[13] Public spaces — spaces

---

networks. Srach, Slovar Sovremennoj Leksiki, Jargona I Slenga ('The Dictionary of Modern Lexic, Jargon and Slang), Academic.

11 Tolerance of the local religious congregations to street art is worth a separate mention. When in 2021 Hamlet created a mural of scissors with a sign "Cut the unnecessary" near Kharkiv's Choral synagogue, the humorous allusion caused criticism on local social networks, but no pushback from the side of the chief rabbi, thus, the mural, like the one near the Catholic cathedral, remained.

12 https://gwaramedia.com/en/cultural-liberation-monument-to-pushkin-dismantled-in-kharkiv/

13 Jacques Rancière, The Emancipated Spectator (London, 2009), p.2–4.

open to the public, unlike our living rooms, however, are very difficult to control, no matter how desirable the idea might be. Painting the mural over was a move that awoke local communities to the infinite possibilities of a grey wall.

By lucky coincidence, Hamlet's exhibition had just opened in the nearby Municipal Gallery, and the audience, walking from this event, experienced the act of painting as a continuation of the gallery display. Walking to their homes, the art lovers decided to take part in the game and film the act. The news spread fast across social media, as the local homeowners were interviewed in situ. On the following day, the 5th of September, the incident was reported by local news 057.ua.[14] And that was how it all began.

---

14 Alena Filippova, 'Eto Schizophrenia: V Zentre Harkova Zalili Kraskoi Graffiti Izvestnogo Hudozhnika' (This is Schizophrenia: A Famous Artist's Graffiti Painted Over in Central Kharkiv), 057.ua, September, 5, 2018, [online].

Fig. 2. "Hui, tak luchshe?" The first comment on the Wall of Discord.

The wall didn't remain grey for long. Soon, an unknown contributor added a commentary, "Hui, tak luchshe?" (the literal translation being 'prick—is that better?') (Fig. 2). Within hours, Kharkiv community services covered the newly emerged obscenity with a layer of grey paint of a different shade. The gesture of wiping the rhetorical question off the wall was seen as an answer by the officials and prompted a follow-up argument (Fig. 3). Positioned strategically on the spot painted over by the communal services, the phrase, "Kharkiv has the Banksy it deserves" ("kakoi Kharkov—takoi i Banksy") hinted at Zinkivsky, who was called "A Kharkiv Banksy" by the media.

Fig. 3. "Kharkiv has a Bansky it deserves"

The two messages were different in style and had different audiences in mind. The first criticised the homeowners' tastes as if saying they should've been happy with the artwork; the second was sooner a critique of Zinkivskiy's own style.[15] That new voice was coming

---

15 The local art community seems to be split in their evaluation of Zinkivskyi's works, two popular bits of criticism include the high number of the artist's works in the historical centre of the city, others point out that Hamlet is not strictly a street artist, as he likes to "freshen up" the murals regularly, in contrast to the laissez-faire philosophy of street art and graffiti, i.e. the understanding of finitude, the ephemeral nature of such art, precisely because it is created in a democratic space of a city. The appearance of an anonymous critic, Zloy Bosch, is indirect evidence of such difference of opinions.

from within the art world, dissatisfied with the level of Kharkiv's art community altogether.

The messages were being swiftly painted over by municipal services, who seemed to have an inexhaustible volume of grey paint in more than 50 shades. It is interesting how readily the services accepted their role. Guarding the wall's grey purity could have been their own interpretation of the broken window policy, their learned wisdom—a clean wall as an example of a well-kept public space.[16] Unfortunately, for the community services, the local public decided to play a different game.

As a child, I had a toy—a self-erasing board where you could draw with a special pencil, then slide an eraser, and all the writing would disappear, making the writing and erasing an infinite process. The Wall of Discord became a live board, fun to draw on exactly because it would inevitably be rubbed out (by municipal services) and then over-written again by the kids (local voices who felt the freedom of anonymity and the pleasure of infinite potential of transformation).

Social media was quick to catch up. Someone would take a photo, and the new message would instantly appear on Facebook and Instagram. The wall even received its own page.[17] The spirit of play and excitement

---

16 Maskaly, Jon, and Lyndsay N. Boggess. "Broken windows theory." The Encyclopedia of Theoretical Criminology (2014), p.1-4.
17 Still active as of December 2024, https://www.instagram.com/wall_of_srach.kharkiv/

gripped the city. The Wall of Discord felt like a two-week festival. Every day, municipal services would paint the wall anew, and every night, another swarm of messages would appear. Between the 5th and 6th of September, a few voices left their opinions about the city aesthetics on the wall, creating a visual conversation, which could be roughly grouped in the following way:

Voice A — Hamlet Zinkivskiy creating his work, 7th Rule;

Voice B — local homeowners erasing the artwork by Zinkivsky;

Voice C — an anonymous supporter of Hamlet, criticising the tastes of the homeowners;

Voice D — municipal services, who, by painting over the emerging signs, wanted to restore the status quo of the wall but who, in fact, helped perpetuate the exchange of thoughts

Voice E — anonymous critics of Zinkivskiy's style (most likely coming from the inside of the artistic community).

By the morning of the 7th of September, the wall became a collage of communal creativity (Fig. 4).

Fig. 4. God asking, "Will you paint me over too?"

The added messages included an advertisement for synthetic drugs—"Fly with us and find yourself" [Улетай с нами и находи себя], two images of penises and a remark in blue paint, saying that "penis is not the end." Written in the Russian language (Hui eto ne konets [Хуй это не конец]), it was a word play, as both "hui" and "konets" are colloquial signifiers of "penis." A visually inconspicuous phrase could be interpreted as a "penis is not a penis." A humorous reference to Rene Magritte's painting, This is Not a Pipe.[18] This voice could have well

---

18 Magritte's "The Treachery of Images" also known as "This is Not a Pipe" painting is a smart re-imagining of figurative art. Rene Magritte, Treachery of Images, 1929, Los Angeles County

belonged to someone who knew art or at least popular culture, which might be supported by Henri Lefebvre's idea that creative classes are the ones most active in urban change.[19] The proximity of Kharkiv State Academy of Design and Arts also makes the neighbourhood a kind of testing ground for the local students to develop their styles.

The most media attention, however, was drawn to an image in the top left corner—a figure reminiscent of Jesus Christ with a question in a speech bubble, "Are you going to paint me over as well?" (Fig. 4) This new message addressed the criticism of the homeowners.

The bubble alluded to the comic book culture that was gaining popularity, the Christ figure—to Charlie Hebdo and a dispute over the censorship of religious images used in non-religious contexts. Located at the intersection of the political and cultural, this message addressed the issue of conservatism in public aesthetics. You might think, "Oh, isn't it too sophisticated an interpretation for what... Kharkiv?" (squint sarcastically). But, first, let us not forget about the inhabitants of the Art Academy nearby, who most definitely studied Magritte. And second, the reference is not unique. Walking near the Kharkiv River in 2018–2021, I bumped into all

---

Museum of Art. Foucault, Michel. This is not a pipe. No. 24. Univ of California Press, 1983.

19 Henri Lefebvre, Writings on Cities, (Blackwell, 1996), p.170-173.

sorts of similar political messages, from "Je Suis Charlie" to a more humorous "Je suis house," making it possible that messages could refer to the notorious Parisian conflict (Fig. 5).[20]

Fig. 5. "Je suis house" Kharkiv River area, 2021

The image could appeal to the homeowners who, the rumours had it, were very religious (nobody knew their religion exactly) and who covered the artwork simply because it was somehow conflicting with their beliefs. Hard to imagine that the homeowners' purported fanaticism could go as far as the Parisian tragedy. Their first statement in the form of painting the mural was also

---

20 https://liveuamap.com/uk/2015/10-january-kharkiv-jesuis charlie-vigil

their last, after which they put up with all of the commotion.

> Anticipating a new iteration of the wall, social media grew more interested in the incident. As of 7th September, a Google search showed at least 33 online articles on the topic. However, with no immediate access to the "wall," mass media became a secondary documentarian, reproducing images outsourced from social media. Social media, in turn, became a first-hand source of information.

The communal services, expectedly, had no trouble painting the god over (their single deity being our mayor, perhaps). Having ended its path on the physical surface of Kharkiv, the god resurfaced in the Internet community of the Wall. In a meme, a bubble coming out of the mouth of a still visible god's face had a sad smile emoji with an exclamation of disappointment—'blia.'[21] (Fig. 6) The meme confirmed the futility of further addressing the homeowners, as their role was taken over by a godless state machine.

---

21 (Short for "bliad," a derogatory term for a sex worker, which today translates more accurately as "fuck" and in this case, might be equated to the English "damn it").

Fig. 6. Covered image with the social media reaction.

With each day the wall events were becoming weirder. On the evening of the 7th of September, two men in civilian clothing appeared near the wall. Showing documents for police services, they said they came to "guard the strategic object" (i.e. the wall). Policy and politics, however, as Jacques Rancière notes, are two opposites, and politics (re-negotiation of rules) calls for opposition to the police, i.e. ones who execute the existing policy.[22] The unexpected intrusion leads to an unexpected result. The men showing identity cards claiming that they represented the state services raised doubts both among social and mass media. Journalists contacted national police and learnt that there had been no official record of the men.[23] Regulations of the Ministry of Internal Affairs

---

22 Rancière, Jacques, Aesthetics and Its Discontents, (Polity Press, 2009).
23 'Kharkovskaya 'Stena Sracha" (Kharkiv 'Wall of Srach'), 112.ua, [news report], 12.09.2019 [online].

that came into force in 2017 prescribe the police to wear uniform on all official calls. The new rules were to create a transparent, rule-based system of relations between citizens and law enforcement that had been compromised by previous political regimes of President Yanukovych and earlier Kuchma.[24] And so, the men weren't treated seriously by either the press or the locals.[25] The affiliation of the newcomers was identified as a parody of the "secret hand of the state." The failed intent to scare the street voices off the wall (that suddenly became the most desired piece of real estate in Kharkiv) was converted into a meme (see Fig. 7).

National news agencies even mistook the meme for physical artwork.[26] Uncovered, the questionable hand of the state retreated and was never seen again. The official police patrol stopped by but, having found no legal grounds for prosecution of anyone or anything, also withdrew, stating to the TSN news agency that they

---

24 The unsolved murder of Georgy Gongadze was one of the stones that crushed public trust in law enformecement services, impacting the urgency of police reform.
Gongadze, Myroslava. "Courage, Service, and the Pursuit of Truth." The International Journal of Ethical Leadership 11.1 (2024), p.20.
25 'Nakaz Pro Zatverdzhennia Pravil Nosinna Odnostroju Polizeiskih' ('Regulation on the Approval of Rules of Wearing Police Uniform'), August, 19, 2017.
26 Olga Skichko, '#stenasracha. Iak u Kharkovi tryvae 'vijna' cheres grafiti i chomu polizia umyla ruki' (#wallofdiscord. In Kharkiv graffiti 'war' continues and why police gave up), TSN, September, 11, 2018.

were aware of the "dispute" but were not planning to "intrude in it any longer."²⁷

Fig. 7. The undercover police

The immediate withdrawal of this murky law enforcement could be the direct result of the recent social changes when, in 2014, Ukrainian civil society called out police brutality, which led to the Maidan protests.²⁸ One

---

27 Ibid.
28 In 2014 during what is now known as the Maidan Revolution, thousands of Ukrainians protested in the main square of Kyiv and in other big Ukrainian cities, including Kharkiv, against then-president Victor Yanukovich's decision to abandon the pro-European course of the country towards strategic alliance with Russia. As a result of the protests Yanukovich had to flee the country. More than 100 protesters in Kyiv died in the clashes with a special police force "Berkut", drawn from a local department and from other industrial centres, particularly from Kharkiv. In February, 2014 Berkut was dissolved by then-Minister of Defence Arsen Avakov. During the fights for

could see a connection between the undercover attempts to police the wall and the spectres of the discredited Berkut task force. The message of the meme was understood by both the authorities and creative voices, leading to the diffusion of the situation from the side of the voices through meme-ification and from the side of authorities via withdrawal.[29] The wall was sanctified as a place of democratic and creative utterances until the public got bored with it, and the artists exhausted their ideas for it, i.e. for another week.

On the 8th of September, two new art techniques appeared: augmented reality and performance, or as Lefebvre would call it, a play of urban creativity.[30] By the 9th of September, the authorities had only one instrument left—the grey paint. Following inertia, they continued to use this instrument until the 10th of September. An unexpected end to the state's involvement in the conversation was brought about by Kharkiv's mayor, Gennady Kernes, who was thought to stand behind the appearance and the subsequent disappearance of the self-proclaimed policemen (Fig. 7). An active user of social networks with over 140,000 followers on Instagram

---

Kharkiv Regional Government Building in March and April, 2014, Kharkiv's Berkut were not allowed to take part in special operations in the city, as Berkut was deemed unreliable, serving the pro-Russian oligarchs. (UN Office of the High Commissioner for Human Rights) (OHCHR). Accountability for killings in Ukraine from January 2014 to May 2016, (July 2016).

29 Wall_of_srach.Kharkiv, September, 8, 2018.
30 Henri Lefebvre, Writings on Cities, (Blackwell, 1996), p.172.

and over 75,000 on Facebook, Kernes wrote a Facebook post in support of Hamlet Zinkivsky. In the post, he addressed communal services and citizens, imploring them not to erase Zinkivsky's art.[31] Kernes stated that "if someone is itching to vandalise Hamlet Zinkivsky's works, they should remember that his art was made not for shallow people, but for the 'genuine Kharkivians.'"[32] We can (and will) say what we want about the man, but he sure knew which direction the popular opinion was bending. The willingness to show he is "with the people" could have been the reason for his choice to communicate via social networks rather than passing a directive through official channels.

The community services concurred and, taking a step further, withdrew from the incident altogether. On the 10th of September, they abandoned their attempts to "police" the wall. A small gesture created a precedent, a new rule for community services. From then on, a new unspoken policy towards street art in Kharkiv was adopted. Starting from the 10th of September 2018, communal services and police have implicitly allowed artists in the city to make street art in daylight.[33] The only

---

31 'Gennady Kernes Zastupilsa Za Gamleta' ('Gennady Kernes Stood Up For Hamlet'), Vgorode, September, 17, 2018.
32 Ibid.
33 Valeria Didenko, 'Mystetztvo U Gromadskih Prostorah: Za i proty' ('Art in Public Spaces: Pro and Contra'), Prostranstvo, July, 2019.

exception was graffiti, which, true to its aesthetics of vandalism, continued to be wiped off the walls.[34]

> The unspoken policy of dividing street art and graffiti, allowing one and banning the other, showed a gap between the laws and unspoken rites of the city. What does one do with street art? — a question that many municipal workers ask themselves in cities across the globe is often solved by creating a habit. Kharkiv communal workers also created their own framework of aesthetics, where they now had to evaluate if the work was art or not and only then proceed to paint it or ignore it. The new rule was very important during the Russian invasion. It is particularly helpful for the street artists who, like the rest of the civilian population, cannot work at night due to the curfew. Some of the works still disappear for various reasons, and we can discuss them at more length with Vasylysa, who has been practising street art in Kharkiv from 2013–2014 and 2022–2024.

Concluding the role of the state in the conflict, two circumstances should be noted. First, the miscommunication between the mayor's message (*"Don't paint over the works of Hamlet Zinkivsky"*) and the reaction of the community services (*"To not paint over any uncommissioned images if they look like art"*). On the surface, it might seem like a gesture of submission, of being intimidated by the power. However, it might also be a display of power on the side of the community services to interpret the mayor's words in a way more comfortable for them. In this way, they preserved their authority over the streets

---

34   Ulrich Blanché, 'Street Art And Related Terms — Discussion and Working Definition', SAUC — Journal Methodologies For Research, V1, N1, (Lisbon, 2015), p.33.

by going over the head of the mayor and creating their own rule. Thus, by surrendering some control over urban aesthetics (allowing figurative street art to pop up), communal services retained their control of communal space overall, as it was them who became the judges of what could now be considered art and what was not. Making an exception for graffiti, which they continued to erase, the community services gained even more power in a way, as they now decide public taste.

Hamlet Zinkivskyi confirmed in a 2019 interview with me that, according to the new unspoken rule, the artist would be left alone (by both police and community services) "as long as it wasn't writing." What of the style of writing or graffiti then? Zinkivskyi, who did not have a high opinion of the artistic values of the local graffiti community, said he added words to his street art because he did not want the images to be interpreted in a wrong way.[35] The need to document, sign and mark art with letters is visible throughout Kharkiv's street art history, and I will speak about it below. Here, though, a question springs to mind, can writing be art? Can it be seen as part of urban aesthetics, and what do community services need to be acquainted with basic font education (or art education at all)?[36] Must art be necessarily

---

35 Ibid.
36 In the same article where he speaks about the relations between children's art, freedom and Kharkiv streets, Mykola Kolomiets also stresses that for many Kharkiv artists, the diary is an important concept. According to Kolomiets, a diary is a way to analyse life when you are in some way restricted in public

augmented with an image if the artist wants to remain on a Kharkiv wall? We once again entered a grey zone between law, human habit and implicit social agreements.

With authorities retreating (having won their private battle), free message exchange continued until the 15th of September. In contrast to repetitive tropes (penis images or obscene language), only several voices brought ideas or communicative methods.

Fig. 8. "Window into the grey world"

On the night of the 8th of September, messages grew rapidly (Figs. 8 and 9). Figure 8 features two artworks. One

---

expression. He mentioned Zinkivskyi and Pavlo Makov as examples of artists working on diaries. https://supportyourart.com/conversations/kolomiets/

is a window signed, "okno v seriy mir" [a window into the grey world]. The other is a flower. Both works have rather symbolic value, as if the authors criticise the homeowners, who supposedly prefer a grey wall (or indeed "world") to free artistic expression. A flower can be interpreted as a symbol of figurative or socialist realist art that people who grew up during the Soviet Union times are supposed to be more accustomed to. This does not mean the homeowners who unwittingly initiated the Wall really were supporters of socialist realist art or of a grey world; we don't even know the reason for them choosing grey paint—most likely, they just had a stock of it at home, accidentally. But when many accidents collide, a pattern might be seen. And so, grey is interpreted here as a negative characteristic of people who do not have an aesthetic taste for art.

Fig. 9. "You're a sun" (amended with "Kernes").

With respect to the established tradition, the grey window was soon filled with penis images. The message on the right of the window said "prodam garazh. Kernes" [Selling a garage. Kernes], as if imitating marketing Voice E while critiquing the mayor. Thus, political Voice H appeared.

Other political utterances followed, including #freesentsov (a Ukrainian film director who at that time was held prisoner in Russia) (Fig. 10). Written in English, the # sign also hinted at the online and international appeal of the Wall. In Fig. 11, we can also see an inscription "stena sracha plachet" [The wall of srach wails]. It is an allusion to the Wailing Wall but also to the Jewish roots of the mayor. In the second image, a paper application offers a number of messages, including ones in English. The appearance of the messages in English suggested new self-awareness. Could that be that international audiences would be interested?

Fig. 10. Application stage

The application technique inspired further political messages, as Voice H used stencils, a technique that allows faster application of the work, i.e. less risk of being caught. The stencil on Fig. 11 features an utterance "clean walls — an illusion of order." It can be both an appeal to the state (Voice C) and local inhabitants (Voice A), alluding to the restrictive nature of cleanliness in a city and the correlation between freedom and dirt.[37] The

---

37 Patrick Joyce wrote about the correlation between liberal, democratic nature of the cities like Paris and the amount of waste/dirt that this freedom allows to be left on the streets. Though the correlation is questioned by others, especially decolonial urban scholars who look at the waste management in former colonial regimes, as Siad Darwish's study on Tunisia https://rucore.libraries.rutgers.edu/rutgers-lib/55422/, there

concept of *cleanliness* might allude to politics as such, which is often considered within the local discursive field to be something "dirty". At the same time, the artists who strive for "clean" or "pure" art might be criticised as living in an illusion. The messages altogether become more political, and aesthetically, these iterations of the wall have a rougher, messier, "dirtier" feel to them.

Fig. 11. "Clean walls are an illusion of order"

is still research that shows a correlation between cleanliness and overly regulated public spaces. Something Kharkiv is definitely complicit in. Joyce, Patrick. The Rule of Freedom: Liberalism and the Modern City. London: Verso, 2003. Pp. 276. Darwish, Siad. "Country of rubbish": waste and the environmental legacies of authoritarianism in post-revolutionary Tunisia. Diss. Rutgers University-School of Graduate Studies, 2017. Campkin, Ben, and Rosie Cox, eds. Dirt: New geographies of cleanliness and contamination. Bloomsbury Publishing, 2012.

The image in Fig. 9 deliberates on the same thought as an apolitical message, 'ti—solnishko' [you are the sun!] is augmented with the surname of the mayor. This addition shows a thin line between apolitical/political. One word separates a very neutral and positive message from a humorous and acutely political one. The game of politicisation/apoliticisation goes on.

The action in Fig. 12, perhaps due to the presence of masked figures, creates a sense of disturbance and aggression, although the banner has an innocent inscription, "Ya za mystetstvo" [I call for art]. In Ukrainian, the message can also be interpreted as "For art I will act...", underlining the strong performativity of the utterance. As previously, it can be seen as a critique of the homeowners, but in a very different style, readiness for an active confrontation. Thus, we can see various kinds and angles of criticism of the wall, with all the participants at one or another becoming an object of criticism—the homeowners, community services, police, Hamlet Zinkivskyi, the Russian Federation (as it always is) and even Kharkiv's mayor.

Fig. 12. "I call for art" action

Not only the messages but the sheer scope of techniques point to a wide range of participants interested in the Wall as a channel of communication. Within a week after the action on the 11th of September, the space lived through a stage of postmodernist art of parody, collage and hypertextualisation (Fig. 9) as the sketches of Hamlet Zinkivsky's original work were attached to the wall (Voice B).[38] There has also been a period of installations, when various objects were put next to the wall, and even art action (voice E) (Fig. 11).

---

38 Mimi Miyoung Lee, Sheng Kuan Chung, 'A Semiotic Reading and Discourse Analysis of Postmodern Street Performance', Studies in Art Education, 51:1, (2009), p.24,

On the 18th of September, the interest in the wall started to fall. As another piece by Hamlet Zinkivsky was painted over in Odesa, the attention of mass media switched to a new location. With 68 remaining in more or less the same state since September 2018, a year later, the wall featured large-scale graffiti in silver-grey tones and an image of a head. Standing out among a series of minor messages was "Velo Troya" (a cycling club in a district of Kyiv called Troyeshina).

Summing up the wall, this microcosm of Kharkiv society, with its political and artistic factions, power play and appeals to the "grey every day" in so many physical and metaphorical ways, one could see even in this seemingly innocent conflict, a snapshot of Ukrainian society that had already accepted the post-Maidan reality, with its new relations with the authorities, becoming voices of the street and being eager to take part in the urban life, even if you are a small minority of people who have paint and aren't afraid to use it.

The Wall of Discord revealed a glimpse of the city's social and aesthetic DNA. Allusions to schizophrenia, grey colour, and literariness (wordplay, allusions, similes, etc.) are all embedded in the history of the city, at times concealed. Street art, this silent instigator of pleasurable chaos, could help us understand what this city has really grown out of.

The Artist and A Window into The Grey World

A year after the Wall of Discord happened and changed our lives forever, on a warm summer day in 2019, I found myself sitting in Gloria. Gloria is one of the two legendary ice cream cafes in Kharkiv (the legend is that its manager once went to Italy and re-imagined Italian gelato by using sour cream instead of the regular one). I sat there silently, praying my blood could process the sugar bomb of the Domino ice cream (Fig 12), as usual. This time, though, I was up for a real treat. I was lucky to meet an enthusiast of local legends who got me in contact with Volodymyr. In his everyday life, Volodymyr was a serious businessman with family, everyday duties and all. In his free time he was a proud biographer of the first street artist of Kharkiv, the legendary madman Oleh Mitasov.

Fig. 13. Domino ice cream, four kinds of ice cream with chocolate and nuts on top, and lemonade at Gloria Cafe.

We are sitting there, and the rabid steppe sun hits the tasselled lemony curtains, and everything — the lemonade with bits of zest, the 1990s songs, and the street outside embraces a light touch of madness as if the entire talk happens in a parallel overlying dimension. Big cities are like this — you always slip into the past and future when stepping into a side door.

Born in the outskirts, Volodymyr lived not conscious of the artsy Kharkiv up until a schoolmate invited him to a party "in the centre."[39] There, circulating amongst the

---

39 "In the centre, let's go to the centre, he/she is central [центровий]" is a Kharkiv descriptor of a status as much as geography. The geography of 'centre' varies depending on where you live, its borders vague and hazy. Growing up in the centre was a sign of elitism, a particular status of a person,

cheap spirits and underground magazines, he was ridiculed, "Don't you know Mitasov? Oh, he's everything." Many of us have been in a situation where the knowledge of a local celebrity marks you as local, "in the circle," cool. And so Volodymyr embarked on the journey of learning the insider language.

For someone who lived in central Kharkiv in the 1990s, Oleh Mitasov was a cult figure. If you knew about him, you were among the "cool kids" who lived or studied in the heart of the city or went to bohemian parties. Even better, if you knew Mitasov, you were likely reading *Sho*, the iconic underground magazine of Ukrainian coolness. *Sho* combined interviews with trendy musicians and photo shoots of the abandoned psychiatric hospitals with thousands of different fonts in one issue. Mitasov's story perfectly fitted into the style of *Sho*, where moody Ukrainian writers in oversized leather jackets from Berlin charity shops wandered the depressingly sepia post-Soviet streets, kicking dead leaves with their dirty trainers. The first generation of independent Ukrainian youth and the first cohort of independent Ukrainian artists could finally decide what their cities should look like. They had absolutely no

---

whose family would be seen as slightly "more Kharkivian", more deserving of the status. In this we never (and for good I think) went through the stage of decentralization that American cities have sustained, as Jane Jacobs noted the tearing of historical community ties back in the 1960s: Jacobs, Jane. "The death and life of great American Cities, Readings in planning theory." London: Jonathon Cape (1962).

money to make any meaningful changes, of course, and so they looked at a story of a madman with a paintbrush covering public walls with jealousy and fascination. His legend was written in their conversations, rumours, and talks, heard and overheard. The tissue of this legend was not unlike the Wall of Discord. Everyone could find or add something important to them.

The Legend

> The legend has it that in the 1990s, there was a man called Oleh Mitasov. He lived in Kharkiv, the capital of wise people and university professors, and dreamt of turning from a wise man into a university professor one day. Many years Mitasov spent at one of the hundreds of Kharkiv colleges, working on his dissertation, which was meant to resolve vital problems of life, i.e. get him an academic salary and pension benefits. When the dissertation was finally completed, he woke up one day, grabbed the only copy of his research, and rushed to the Highest Attestation Committee (BAK) to submit it. A typical scholar that he was, though, Mitasov was extremely absent-minded and, in the rush, left the only copy of his dissertation on a tram. The tram tossed and drifted and disappeared from view. Years of research were gone, devoured by the city. Mitasov never recovered from the shock, went mad and started going about the city centre, covering the walls with scribbles from his study. His most popular quotations of his were, understandably, *BAK* and "Kharkiv where? On Earth."

The whole legend of Mitasov speaks about the city more than the man. Mitasov himself was not really a scholar, but many people who studied at nearby universities and lived among his writings were. It was for them, the hundreds of long-suffering academics, for whom the abbreviation BAK came in the horror dreams.

Being a regular cliche, I once also tried to write a PhD thesis at V N Karazin National University. Between department meetings and roaming dark university hallways, the words were flying into my ears, "You need to have a publication in a BAK collection; only BAK publications really count." BAK collections [ВАКовська збірка] were the equivalent of Western peer-reviewed journals (only without peers or any reviews), and it was essential and great bureaucratic pain to get published in one of those badly assembled books meant for the shelves of university libraries across Ukraine. Not finishing my dissertation was also a rite of passage. In 2014, the head of our department got into a corruption scandal and fled to Russia; the whole system seemed to be rotten, and abandoning it was my kind of revolt, but also a typical gesture of a local student, which Mitasov's legend reflected.[40]

It is known that every bohemian person (or a corrupted politician) in Kharkiv needs to start a PhD. Finishing it is not necessary. The incomplete nature of research is, in

---

40 I didn't really go to Maidan, and will always regret that. I would take a trolley bus every morning from the Freedom square to go to the endocrinology department where I was treated then, and going past the protests unfolding in front of the regional administration, my medicated body would feel sorrow and weakness, which would later spill into an outburst of social activism that lasted for six years to come. Revolutions are interesting in this way.

fact, advisable (it harmonises well with the ever-unfinishable nature of street art, the street, or the city itself). Mitasov's dissertation story in this context is likely saying more about the fandom than the street artist himself ("not-an-artist", I naturally mean).

It can also be seen as a homage to the most famous art project of late 20th century Kharkiv — Boris Mikhailov's *Unfinished Dissertation*. As we all know, all good artists lived in Ukraine, and all the great ones in Kharkiv. Like Pavlo Makov, Boris Mikhailov is an exceptional figure in Ukrainian art — a genius photographer who turned photographic film from a utilitarian tool of Soviet realist documentation into art. Distorting, manipulating, and playing with the film in all the ways that were not allowed and therefore not possible under the Soviets, Mykhailov was deepening the cracks in the already crumbling totalitarianism. Through these cracks the inherent weirdness of Kharkiv came through.

Every city is weird in its own special way. Kharkiv's weirdness can be seen in the half-naked men always circulating the Botanical Gardens and in the fishermen angling tin cans from the dirty, shallow city rivers. In the strange obsession with higher education, Mykhailov humorously captured these tiny weirdnesses, as Kharkiv is always humorously weird. Kharkiv laughs at life like a pair of seagulls in a high-pitched ultrasound kind of way.

The *Unfinished Dissertation* is a joke in itself. It is a parergon. One where notes on the fringes and the entire life of the author are plastered over academic pages to the point where not a single line of the original paper can be seen. It is a photo album of Kharkiv's everyday life, enriched with Mikhailov's reading lists, notes and diary entries that frame the images, deliberately 'unqualified' for a serious exhibition or portfolio. Repurposed photographs could be easily written over and reimagined, following the local myth of an unsuccessful dissertation. In a way, Mikhailov and most of the Kharkiv School of Photography dive into art by abandoning a plethora of Kharkiv's technical colleges where they were getting their education. Out of multiple explanations, why the starting point for all of these people was technical could be the state of humanities, their status, and the general suspicion of the Soviet state towards humanities. Technical education gave a Soviet citizen access to the instruments and a dose of welcome anonymity.[41]

The Kharkiv School of Photography plays with the myth of an educational institution as a

---

[41] My mum, who always dreamt of becoming an historian, like her grandfather, nearly gave the family a heart attack in late 1970s, and was sent to study economics instead. Grandpa, as it happens, was executed for being Stalin's enemy of the state, when he was a 3rd year student at Kharkiv University. History was seen as a dangerous subject. More on the connection between science and Kharkiv School of photography: Nadiia Bernard-Kovalchuk. Scientific Imagery Re-Coded: The Appropriation of Scientific Photography Aesthetics in The Late Soviet Non Official 'Creative' Photography — The Case of Oleg Maliovany. Umění, 2022, LXX (3), p.312—324.

place/power/structure, as it exists outside of any defined place or institution. It is a school like a school of thought. Even the styles of its representatives are so different that the only point of crossing is a "Kharkiv" relationship between the city and a photographer. Being a drop-out in this ever-unfinished Kharkiv becomes a school and a university where aspiring artists find growth in certain aesthetics. Cultural memory and continuity play a tremendous role here, perhaps precisely because cultural communities feel the lack, the missing gap.

The Shilo group who thought about the problems of continuity in the Kharkiv School of Photography, declared their connection with the local tradition by 'completing' Mikhailov's dissertation (perhaps, to his displeasure even). Their aim in the project was precisely the aching wound of continuity.[42] In the multiple unfinished and finished dissertations of this city, locals embracing local history pronounced the following,

---

42 "Вопрос преемственности нас постоянно беспокоил, и для того, чтобы у «Школы» появился фундамент, мы даже сделали специальный проект — «закончили» «Неоконченную диссертацию» Михайлова. После этого жеста стало сразу легче работать. [The question of continuity was constantly bothering us, and in order for the school to get a foundation, we even made a special project — "finished" Mikhailov's Unfinished Dissertation. This gesture immediately made the work so much easier.] https://birdinflight.com/ru/vdohnovenie/opyt/gruppa-shilo-ironiya-eto-chisto-harkovskaya-shtuka.html

> We see you, the city, and you, the city, see us. We remember what the city was before through the eyes of those who came before us. We remember the erased and the forgotten. We cherish and bring to the surface what has been concealed, we speak of the unspoken.

The academic legend was disproved by local artists, students and employees of the Kharkiv State Academy of Design and Fine Arts. The windows of the academy overlooked Mitasov's apartment building, and then students like Ira Olenina would often bump into Mitasov, who would either ask for paint, spill various sorts of enigmatic pearls of wisdom, or just creep out female students. Yet, disproving the legend never helps, as much as it creates other parallel legends. Like with the Wall of Discord, the becoming a legend, a shared text, the story evades authorship, slips between the fingers and just refuses to be finished. Every new co-author can re-actualise it, linking to the events that are currently important for the city.

In 2019, my friend Viktoriia Ivanova and I were sitting in a coffee shop—the normal third-wave one this time, with vegan desserts, black filter coffee and bored-looking baristas, thinking of the most popular Kharkiv stories we could write about. The tall windows of the coffee shop overlooked the famous abandoned house known as the Roof of the World (Fig. 13).[43] Its mesmerising skeleton gave us the idea to make a series of stop-

---

[43] In 2022 I saw a video by a foreign blogger who presented the long-abandoned Roof as the victim of the Russian aggression.

motion animations that would humorously re-imagine some of the popular legends of Kharkiv. Naming the series *Kharkiv Legends*, we immediately decided that one of the first episodes would be dedicated to Mitasov. Back then, we, the seasoned Kharkivians, naively thought that this figure was well forgotten (despite the fact we both went to an exhibition dedicated to him a year before). Forgotten meant that we could really play with the plot, adding the most ridiculous details. When the animation premiered at a local film festival, Bardak [Mess], we gathered at our friend's place with the Metaphysical Cinema club for a discussion. To my surprise, the first question was, "Do you think you used Mitasov's trendiness to get famous?" I was absolutely struck by the idea that after a quarter of a century, such a figure could be seen as trendy. But, in a way, Mitasov continued to inhabit our shared urban imagination, not unlike the Roof of the World.

In a way, it probably was, victim of abandonment and forgetfulness that post-colonial societies struggle to get out of.

Fig. 14. Roof of the World, Kharkiv, June 2023.

When a year later, we finished our stop-motion animation short dedicated to Mitasov, our idea was to channel this transition from a silent city to an outspoken one. The plot wove itself around the feeling we got wandering around Mitasov's former apartment block. Nooks and arches, abandoned red brick mansions and the beautiful Ukrainian Moderne School of Industrial Art and Design. Stray cats and hills overlooking the lower city behind the Kharkiv River. Deciphering the faded white paint of Mitasov's methodical writing, we felt the burden of the erased layers of history, his ever-lasting suspicion and madness. The plot of the animation ended up revolving around Mitasov writing the secrets of the crumbling Soviet regime across the city. When the last hidden, concealed and erased secret is painted over, the USSR falls apart, giving way to the free Ukrainian spirit.

We had very little idea what Mitasov's stance towards Ukrainian independence actually was. Chances are, he didn't care that much, but he channelled the surrounding nervousness into his public writings unconsciously. It was rather the way we, the first independent generation, experienced the falling of the Soviet Union as a disentanglement from the lie of this failed political formation.

The story of the secret police, however, wasn't a figment of my imagination. Back at Gloria Ice Cream café, Volodymyr sipped a lemonade the colour of a toxic lemon and told the story about Mitasov from the most unusual angle,

> "Kharkiv is, of course, the city of the Earth," he said, making sure as he glanced at me that I was obviously informed of that universal fact. "Masons curate four cities in Ukraine. Kharkiv belongs to the earth, of course, because it is a city of the militia." I continued to nod, though my brain was struggling. But then, I started to perceive Volodymyr's story as a piece of art in itself, and the puzzles fell into their rightful places (I also started to get a kick from the acidity of the lemonade).

Volodymyr went on, telling me about Mitasov, who was brought up in a family of KGB agents, who not only inflicted innumerable psychological, moral and physical damage to the citizens of Kharkiv (rumours had it, they destroyed a church in the courtyard of their house because it took up a place that could be used for garages). With all of the concealed baggage, they raised their children in an atmosphere of silencing and secrets. When the Soviet Union started to crack, all of these secrets accumulated in the unconsciousness of Mitasov and began spilling onto Kharkiv walls. Like a broken Word file, Mitasov's writing was impossible to decipher, but it was clear that something vital could be encrypted there,

Fig. 15. Writings on Oleh Mitasov's house (likely to be his, but there have also been many imitations in the area), 2019

"Where is Kharkiv?"
"On Earth."
"No," Volodymyr corrected me. "On the land. Soil. The soil is all that Kharkiv is about. It is the city of the soil, green, and therefore, 'mentovskyi gorod' [the city of militiamen]. Why do you think the Soviets have all those Mother-LAND figures (he said the word in English for us to fully comprehend the worldwide consequences of the information)? It's their pagan goddess. Soviet secret services were very pagan this way. They didn't like Christ much." He mentioned that in 2014, after the beginning of the war and the annexation of

Crimea, he also felt the energy of the secret services' paganism moving from the north.

Fig. 16. Ibid

With the second helping of the radioactively yellow lemonade at Gloria, it all started to sound suspiciously logical. My colleague understood the danger and swiftly invited us all to freshen our heads on a walk to Oleh Mitasov's house. There, looking for the signatures that remained, I was getting more and more why Mitasov and the Wall of Discord could be phenomena of a similar nature. One, a legendary madman; another, the wall of an electric booth, entailed the vibe of local urban aesthetics and unconsciousness. The liberating spirit of anonymity, the tool through which everyone, Volodymyr, me, Pavlo Makov, Hamlet Zinkivskyi, or a lady working in community services, could express our own understanding of the city.

Not accidentally, none of the professional artists allow a thought of Mitasov as an actual artist. To be an artist, they laugh, you need to have a clear intention, and Mitasov was barely present in this world. At the same time, his style and the audacity to paint in public spaces influenced many of these professional artists, even if they find it difficult to admit. He was also most likely sensitive to the division between public and private, as the style of his writing differed in the apartment, in the hallways, and outside. Something was inspiring, something sexy in the idea that all you needed for self-expression was a bucket of paint.

Street artists started their careers by imitating Mitasov's style; students of the local Academy of Applied Arts and Design wrote a dissertation about Mitasov's unfinished dissertation. Pavlo Makov collected furniture from Mitasov's apartment and organised the first exhibition dedicated to this figure in his own studio. The exhibition of Mitasov's furniture at the Municipal Gallery was also a result of a new generation of artists, such as Konstiantyn Zorkin, getting to the cellars of the gallery in order to "sort out old histories," see what was there and create additional space for exhibitions. For a non-artist, in fact, Mitasov had a surprising number of exhibitions, notably two via Makov, including one in the Pinchuk Art Centre and one in the Municipal Gallery in 2018. Besides, his works were integrated into the art practices of Makov (a board game he worked on) and in street art by Hamlet Zinkivskyi. Both Zinkivskyi and Makov participated in the Venice Biennale at various times. Something that would look impressive in anyone's portfolio.

It isn't new for famous artists to inhale the spirits of the streets and get inspired by the raw flesh of urban unconsciousness. Yet, it is not often that such explorations jumpstart a legend so sticky it lives for decades. In 2018, there was an exhibition dedicated to Mitasov in the Municipal Gallery, the same place where the 7th Rule was shown the same year. Pieces of the furniture from the not-an-artist's former flat were stored in the cellars of the gallery for years, like ghostly spirits leaking into the dreams of new generations.

In his interview with me in 2019, Hamlet Zinkivskyi mentioned that 2014 changed a lot in his attitude to the city. Before Maidan, he was thinking of leaving. Yanukovych's corrupt governing style started to tighten the knot; it felt like there wasn't much air left in Kharkiv. The protests against developers were losing. Most notoriously, the building of a highway that cut through Kharkiv's Central Park in 2010 broke the green belt of the city alongside activists' hopes. The Revolution of Dignity changed this. More people started to participate in urban life more readily. Rather than migrating and building a gallery artist career, Zinkivskyi went onto the streets of Kharkiv with the ever-expanding mission of covering the city with his art. Like him, other artists started to feel less likely to be arrested for their nightly ventures, and the walls started to talk through various styles and philosophies.

Electrified by the revolution, Kharkiv started to reconnect with its multiple silenced pasts, either through Mitasov or through taking part in shared thought exchanges on Gogol Street. While in the 1990s, Oleh Mitasov walked along the streets of central Kharkiv with paint and brush as a cover for his mental condition, now the liberty of doing something on the street was open to many more, from professional artists to amateur enthusiasts. The freedom to create ends only with the freedom of someone else to dislike and cover up. While being called "schizophrenic," the artwork and the discord that proceeded were, in fact, a very conscious and surprisingly grown-up discussion of the local public community.

PS. As you can see, The Wall of Discord — oh, let's be honest, it's a Wall of Sratch — produced a place in which the aesthetic unconscious of the city came out from the dreams of all the voices that dared to speak their mind. From the liberating power of street writing that came with the slow decomposition of the Soviet straightjacket to the actual hospital straightjacket and the city balancing between a closed cell and an open case in psychiatry. Finally, it gave us a chance to talk about the notorious Kharkiv's greatness in its multilayered dream. The results of the Wall's heavenly emergence were to bring these and other questions that bother city dwellers about freedoms and responsibilities to create and clean up, of how to retake the grey city myth and make it your own. The Wall was a result, importantly, of ignited interest of Kharkiv's creative communities in the city; the way it looked suddenly became part of the responsibility of the communities, a democratic manifestation from ridiculing undercover servants of the law to making fun of the mayor, to the ultimate cry for international justice in #freesentsov tag. The Wall was serious and funny, humorous and nostalgic, interactive and included a whole lore of AR, documented by a kind unknown who set up an Instagram page of the Wall, which hopefully we will continue to enjoy for more years to come.

I would not go as far as to say that the protection of Kharkiv by its people in 2022 was a result of the Wall. It wasn't, surely. But the Wall fixed a moment between the time when a small activist community fought for Central Square to the empowered, active majority that stood up for Kharkiv eight years later.

The city is always a work in progress, a fleeting butterfly changing its wings. It balances the desire to change and a wish to preserve its hidden myths and legends, which form the spine of the city. The spine of Kharkiv has been formed by many generations of architects and styles, imperial and Soviet, hidden and overtly Ukrainian. Its text continues, and flesh grows on the skeleton. In my fevered dreams, as I wake up reading about another explosion or seeing it in my window, my body stiffens, my heart jumps, and my pulse beats in my eardrums. Kharkiv becomes a little bit less bodily and a little more of a fevered nightmare. And yet, the city known to me and many other infinitely more informed scholars, Kharkiv, exists online, in our writings, in the structure of our skeletons that repeat its rivers' flow (as Pavlo Makov suggests). And we are all Kharkiv, and we are all a dream. And we will come back, hopefully, for the future Kharkiv, the city of justice, freedom and all kinds of beautiful buildings.

Coffee break

The Last Walk

From Hjørdis

Dear Viktoriia and Vasylysa
The story about the Wall of Discord is hilarious, Viktoriia! To me, there's something quintessentially Ukrainian about it. The way the neighbours took the matter in their own hands and simply painted over the artwork (I assume no formal complaints were filed). The witty comments about society, politics, and art by the art community. The opportunism by the advertisers. And the ad hoc way the city administration tried to handle it. The directness and informality of it all.

I can't help but wonder what went through the minds of the neighbours who painted over the artwork in the first place. Which emotions and associations did it evoke in them? Or maybe it was not the artwork itself they were upset about. Maybe they felt that their space was invaded? Maybe they felt threatened by an increasingly strong movement of young liberals? Maybe they would indeed have preferred "Hui"?

The story reflects the power of the artistic community in Kharkiv. They actually managed to change the laws about street art in Kharkiv. I wonder if the story would have been the same if it had happened in 2013? It seems to me that the art activists were more concerned about the negative consequences of the city administration and law enforcement back then.

When I did my fieldwork with Vasylysa and her friends in Kharkiv in 2013, we mainly did innocent projects that did not in any way attract the attention of the authorities. We did master classes, movie and discussion nights, and we designed and installed birdhouses around the city. There was one event, however, that created several opportunities to interact with law enforcement officers. It was a protest in the format of an art intervention called "The Last Walk." I know that that event was particularly meaningful to you, Vasylysa. Maybe you can say a bit about why it stood out to you from the other projects we did with AA?

This is how "The Last Walk" happened:
The art installation was prompted by an aggravating decision of the city administration to build a church in the park called Dzerkalney Strumin' in the centre of Kharkiv across from the Opera House.

Someone had called for a protest, and AA showed up along with a crowd of unhappy neighbours, students, and activists on that cold November evening in 2013. There were maybe 60 people altogether shouting a range of different slogans like, "Stop destroying the park!" and "Give back joy to the people! Give back the park!" We were standing in front of newly erected green fences that isolated about one-third of the park from the rest. The sound of lorries and chainsaws inside the fences most certainly drowned out the sound of our voices. On the outside, though, we had a pretty good time coming up with rhythmic slogans and getting everyone to shout along.

At some point during the protest, Vasylysa turned to the other members of AA and said: "I am 22 years old. Ukraine has been independent for 22 years. We are the first generation to speak up, to refuse to keep our mouths shut." She then suggested protesting against the church construction by putting up 22 life-sized figures of styrofoam in the park: 21 of them with black tape over their mouths and the last one without. This is how "The Last Walk" was born.

Two days later we met in AA's workshop to cut out the styrofoam silhouettes and tape them to sticks so they could be put in the ground. All the members of AA were there, along with about five artists from the local art community. The following day, we went to Dzerkalney Strumin to put up the figures. This is when we met the police for the first time. They sent us home with the message that we needed permission to protest. Five days later, we returned with a stamped and signed permission. The police officers also returned and told us to leave once again. The person from our group who had received the permission was not able to take part in the protest because he had left the city the day before to join Maidan in Kyiv. Another four days passed, and we returned for the third time with our figures and a new permission signed by Danylo, who was present at the protest. At this point there were only three of us left. The same police officers met us in the park and told us to leave again. This time, their reasoning was about the wording in the permission. According to them, we did not have the right to put up the figures and leave them there; we would have to stand in the park with the installation the entire day.

"To people, this is rubbish," the police officers told us. "It is an art installation!" Vasylysa promptly replied. "It is rubbish!" "It is art!" I remember recording the conversation and smiling under my scarf. It would have been funny if the situation hadn't been so absurd and such a disappointing reminder of a deliberately hostile system.

At this point, the silhouettes were pretty beaten up, so we installed them in the rubbish bins in the park. The police officers got it their way, but we did leave a note about the ridiculous process on a bin for the curious observers to read.

To me, "The Last Walk" was meaningful because we were out there, confronting the system that represented the mindset we wanted to change. It was civil society claiming a voice and standing up to the authorities.

In Kyiv, though, Maidan had started, and similar sentiments were expressed there, however, on a much larger scale. I travelled between Kharkiv and Kyiv at the weekends to take part in the Maidan protests. Returning to Kharkiv after those visits seemed a bit disappointing to me. The energy and the unity on the streets of Kyiv were undetectable to me in Kharkiv. After a visit to Kyiv I noticed that the newspaper headlines in the kiosks were not representing the movement on Maidan truthfully. One newspaper had a picture of Maidan with a couple of people protesting, saying, "Where did Maidan go?" I had just been there, demonstrating with tens of thousands of protesters. I understood then that there were strong forces at play to keep the voices down in Kharkiv and that the two cities were positioned quite differently in general.

Hjørdis

How I met Shevelyov

From Vasylysa
Dear ladies, thank you. Your conversation led me to the way I heard about another scholar from Kharkiv, Shevelyov, for the first time. That was another episode of Kharkiv's public space transformations.

It was due to the plaque in memory of Shevelyov that was installed in Kharkiv in 2013. The plaque was destroyed shortly after its installation in September 2013. Rumours were drifting in the air that he was a nationalist. In March 2014, I saw blood for the first time on Kharkiv's streets. I was turning from Yaroslava Mudroho str. into Sumska str. while talking over the phone to my friend B. We spoke Ukrainian. A few moments later, I saw people dragging people out of the Regional Administration Building. They were beaten and forced to walk on their knees towards the Monument of Lenin that had been standing there until September 2014. People on their knees were Euromaidan activists whom I was about to join for my daily shift. They were beaten for their pro-Ukrainian position. Being Ukrainian was as dangerous as it gets back then, as it is now, in December 2024, when I am reading Shevelov in a warm bathtub at the Quiet Center under the sound *of an air raid alarm. It is still crazy to think that back in 2013, Shevelov's writing was still passed quietly from person to person, as a secret document, or foreign erotica magazines (I guess this is how I imagine it was back in the Soviet Union when he was active). Today, in Kharkiv, going to Shevelov's apartment to read or buy his books is part of the new normal. However, personally, I still feel the price for this change was paid by those activists who crossed the Svodody Square on their knees in the cold March of 2014 and whose blood I documented on a photo that I still store on my hard drive.*

I do think this example, as well as The Last Walk installation and the Wall of Discord, are parts of the larger process of taking the right to the city into our own hands. And as you, Hjørdis, asked me why I consider this event particularly important in AA's history, it is due to the fact that this story has brought together various social bubbles. As you mentioned, we were joined by artists, but also friends and colleagues from other professional fields. I consider this an important experience of coming together. Just like the night of the blood drops, that afternoon at the rubbish bins, something shifted so that I am able to reflect on it only now.

Vasylysa

Shevelovs legends

From Viktoriia

Dear both,
I'm glad you mentioned Shevelov, Vasylysa. He's a very relevant scholar to Kharkiv. A city native, he was born in 1908 but had to leave in 1943, the previous time the big war came

into the city. He had to leave because the city was occupied, and Shevelov felt it was occupied twice over — by Nazi Germany and Soviet Russia. He returned to Kharkiv only when we became independent but spent his entire life working to make sure that it would happen. His story is very much your story, too, the spilling of Ukrainian culture far beyond this city and, at the same time, a return to Kharkiv as a source of energy, inspiration and love. I'm not a Shevelov biographer, but, like you and like many other Kharkivians, I've become mesmerised by this figure to the extent I feel our book will be impossible without a short introduction of him and his views. Also, because Kharkivians would absolutely demolish us if we don't, haha. So, here are two legends about the menace of all imperial professors, the one and only Yuri Shevelov.

Shevelyov's Legends — Legend One — How to Become a Ukrainian

One day, when Yuri/George Shevelov was a teenager, he noticed his sister's boyfriend, Anatolii Nosov, with a book. It was Mykhailo Hrushevskyi's *History of Ukraine*, and, knowing that Nosov spoke Ukrainian, Shevelov decided, in a very teenage way, to be a pain and said that though the Ukrainian language existed, it was "ugly" (so they said at school, perhaps), and therefore absolutely useless. Nosov looked at him calmly and answered that a language that millions of people speak cannot be ugly. And what do you know, three decades later, at Harvard, Professor Shevelov is writing a book on the history of the Ukrainian language. Jump to 2013, Kharkiv, and in the middle of the night, the memorial plaque to Yuri Shevelov, "one of the greatest Ukrainian linguists of the 20th century," is smashed in the Salamander house, where Shevelov grew up because of his being "a Ukrainian nationalist."

The city changes, and so do its citizens. Some cities, however, forget what was before or are made to forget. One of the most violent stories I've heard happened in 1933. When one of the founders of Ukrainianization, Mykola Skrypnyk, shot himself in that fancy office of his in Derzhprom, sensing the approaching purges, his little son was taken to 're-education.' The son's name was changed to Russian, and he was re-educated into a model Russian Soviet man. During my pedagogic course at Kharkiv National University, we were made to read the *Pedagogical Poem* written by "one of the greatest Soviet educators," Anton Makarenko, who established an 'employment commune' for difficult children (it was essentially a labour camp with perks). We were never told that Anton Makarenko, an ethnic Ukrainian himself, was the one who re-educated, i.e. Russified Ukrainian children, including Skrypnyk's son.

What does George Shevelov have to do with this? Shevelov was a linguist, a literary scholar, and a historian of language. Essentially, he was an archaeologist of knowledge in the way Foucault was. Shevelov's entire life was dedicated to remembering all that Ukrainian culture that existed and was erased. The corpus of his texts holds myriads of stories about the development of Ukrainian identity, about Kharkiv.

In 1991, as Oksana Zabuzhko recalls, George Shevelov made his first speech in Ukraine before his colleagues when he received the Taras Shevchenko National Prize. Looking at a hall full of yesterday's Soviet nomenclature, Shevelov started his speech with the words,

"My dear friends, and honorable enemies!"[44]

This phrase, Zabuzhko said, stunned the audience—such honesty in a public speech was unthinkable in the USSR. For many people in the audience it was that night and those words that made it clear that the Soviet Union was over. Like no one else, George Shevelov had been preparing for this moment his entire life. He believed and remembered for us four different eras of Kharkiv, four cycles of violence and hope.

Legend 2. The Fourth Kharkiv

1st Kharkiv —
of the fortress and Cossacks who guarded the Free Land

2nd Kharkiv —
of provincial dullness and trade, coal and bread

3rd Kharkiv —
of the rebels with transparent blue eye-lashes

4th Kharkiv —
of Soviet dolls who forgot how to speak

---

44 It could have well been a linguistic equivalent of "Guess who's back, b-ches!" on Shevelov's part.
Шевельов Ю. Вибрані праці : у 2 кн. Кн. І. Мовознавство [упор. Л. Масенко] / Юрій Шевельов. — К.: Вид. дім «Києво-Могилянська Академія», 2008, p.448

> 5th Kharkiv —
> of us all, strong and weak

In 1948, Shevelov wrote an essay, "The Fourth Kharkiv." Like all the ground-breaking texts in this world, it was meant to be a modest review of a little-known book by Leonid Lyman, *A Tale About Kharkiv* (if you find three people who have read this novel, you're surrounded by Ukrainian geeks, beware). Shevelov's review not only outgrew the reviewed novel but laid a foundation for the way Kharkivians see their own city today.

It is an elegant dissection of time in a city that is colonised yet fighting back. Shevelov looks at the way two different colonising structures (the Russian Empire and the USSR) built the systems of memory erasure, domination and "soft violence."[45] Like soft power, soft violence has an accumulative power, impacting the generations to come. The soft violence of the Russian Empire and, later, the Soviet Union towards Ukrainian culture was founded on the concept of invisibility. Ukrainian culture was not to be seen or spoken about with the wider world. Even such Ukrainian authors as Mykola, aka "Nikolai" Gogol, who during his lifetime gained fame for his Ukrainian texts (*Taras Bulba* was his main best-seller) have not been represented and translated abroad. Russian departments across the globe continue to teach only the "Russian writer Gogol", thinking of his essential Ukrainian style — absurdist humour, baroque

---

45 Shevelov didn't use this term, in fact, I've just made it up to describe the theme of his essay.

word-building, and syntax—as accidental orientalist quirks. The lack of translations of his Ukrainian texts originates from the lack of resources, which the Russian and Soviet states naturally preferred to direct at the texts that would display, even if in very talented forms, the greatness of the "Russian world."[46]

The soft violence of erasure and invisibility followed Ukrainian culture, even in the cities where Ukrainian art got its main inspirations. Kharkiv, the home of the legendary Honcharivka, of which Hrihorii Kvitka so eloquently wrote in 1836, by the end of the 19th century, was turned into a bleak provincial Russian city.[47] How? Why? George Shevelov painstakingly deconstructs the slow violence of the empire and its perpetual attempts to level, hide and conceal the differences, individuality, and originality of others.

The fourth Kharkiv starts with Ïvga, a character by Hrihorii Kvitka and the first Cossack-free Kharkiv, walking into the Second Kharkiv. She feels like she is suffocating in the crowd "with no one to speak to." Some soldiers didn't let her into a church, a thing that

---

46 Be a rebel—read Gogol's *Ukrainian Dykanka* cycle! (Evenings Near the Village of Dikanka; Myrhorod).
47 Hryhorii Kvitka-Osnovianenko (1778-1843) was a Ukrainian writer, one of the first who published in contemporary Ukrainian language, known as the "father of Ukrainian prose" on par with Ivan Kotlyarevsky, father of Ukrainian drama. Kvitka's seminal texts The Witch of Konotop (1833); Marusia (1832), The Courtship at Honcharivka (1835), and other place Kharkiv, and wider East of Ukraine on the world literary map. He was also a head of Kharkiv's aristocracy (1817-1828).

would be unimaginable for the Ukrainian identity, where the church was considered a place of congregation and community. The space of the 19th century Kharkiv, a Russified provincial city of an empire, is divided into clear casts, where being Ukrainian should be hidden under an official attire. The Ukrainian Revolution of 1917-19 brings a new tide–the wild writers and revolutionaries from the Wild Field.[48] If Russian Soviet higher-ups made Kharkiv a capital, "we will make it [a] Ukrainian capital of our Ukrainian Ukraine," these revolutionaries pronounced. The majority of these bright vagabonds with "blue transparent eye-lashes" were buried in Sandarmokh ravine in 1937, executed as enemies of the 'great Russian People' (which they probably were by virtue of being non-Russian).

The fourth Kharkiv, described by Leonyd Lyman in his WWII novel, didn't know about their predecessors. The children of the vagabonds with blue transparent lashes didn't study the texts of those vagabonds at school. This generation of youngsters was quiet, sneaking, frozen, afraid to speak of the future or change, and apolitical. It was a generation of survivors of three genocides — by the Soviets and Nazis, and the Soviets again. These Kharkivians lied and twisted and turned to adapt

---

[48] The Wild Field (or The Wild Fields) is a part of the natural landscape of the Ukrainian East and South-East, also known as steppe — vast fields of grassland, and an important cultural trope for the Ukrainian historical identity. It was the habitat of Ukrainian cossacks. Mykola Gogol in Taras Bulba gives a poetic description of this rich soil (chornozem) flatlands.

and survive in the impossible Sovietness. They didn't know and didn't want to know about the existence of the Ukrainian Ukraine and Kharkiv, its Ukrainian capital. They could survive a nuclear catastrophe, but wouldn't survive the truth told their faces.

Shevelov analyses this generation of the fearful citizens of the Fourth Kharkiv, trying to find inside them a grain of hope for the future—the possibility of a Fifth Kharkiv.

And here we are. The Fifth Kharkiv, singing Ukrainian carols under Russian bombs in the winter of 2024 in a merchant cellar built during the Second Kharkiv on the oldest street of the former fortress of the First Kharkiv (today, it carries the name Hrihorii Kvitka-Osnovianenko). On our right shoulder sits the Third Kharkiv of the executed rebels. They whisper: hold on, stand up to the bully, build a new Ukraine. On our left shoulder are the fearful Fourth Kharkivians, whispering: just survive, no matter how, occupied or not, just survive.

But we don't want to *just survive* anymore. We are fed up with the world treating us like slaves. We were born free. We want to live bright and bold. The sixth Kharkiv was too close (though we could discuss if the sixth Kharkiv necessarily means another cycle of oppression). The sixth Kharkiv drove a stray Russian tank through our main streets and was burnt in a school along Taras Shevchenko Street in early 2022, very fittingly, just like Taras told us to in his testament. We felt the freezing breath of the Russian world in an unmarked grave in the forest of Izyum, where Volodymyr Vakulenko, a children's writer, was found, shot and killed. The sixth Kharkiv was breathing down our neck. The neo-imperial Russian city where prisoners would be made to sing Soviet WWII songs mixed with the Russian Imperial Anthem on a morning line-up before a shooting squad. Maybe we have already skipped that terrifying future and are on our Seventh Kharkiv? The Kharkiv of Zechariah, the Seventh Eye, the Memory of God? We might not be there just yet, still trying to embrace Shevelov's four Kharkivs. But we continue to sing a military Ukrainian carol (just like 100 years back, raising money for our army, as we have an army now! We are not defenceless anymore) in a friendly wine cellar with Christmas lights and candles, hiding from the Russian bombs in Kharkiv, in the year 2024.

On health

11.02.2025, Berlin

Dear Viktoriia,
As I read your text, I feel each letter, each story through my body. Somehow, it feels that talking about the body, or better yet, embodied experience, is as trendy as it gets, at least among the Berlin art community, which is interesting and infuriating at the same time. As you know, I got recently kicked out from a discussion at the famous Berlin Contemporary Art Centre, which is dedicating itself to serving as a platform for

dialogue; however, the dialogue seems to be strictly prohibiting speaking about the ongoing war and what my bodily experience brings into the cosy artsy rooms. This dissonance between the lived reality in Kharkiv and in Berlin over the last three years often feels schizophrenic to me, or, as it's trendy to say, bipolar. As the larger public starts to speak more about the importance of mental health, I feel it might be a good opportunity for an honest discussion, which would allow the texts you shared here to be embedded in libraries across the world, which would achieve the dream of the many Kharkiv'yanyn, and human beings as such — to be seen, to be heard, and to participate in the global dialogue, and not be hidden under the blanket, when things get a bit too raw and therefore, a bit too ugly, to face them.

I thank you for your work, and I am deeply grateful for the day Tanya connected us. Kharkiv is connecting people, those who are ready to dive into the depths of the unconscious. It's a dangerous but exciting journey.

Sorry if my text sounds a bit esoteric; it's just that, as you know, I am on a second round of angina, so antibiotics might be speaking for me right now. As an artist, I take this as a sign of another artistic experience, as in Kharkiv, I was treated with augmentin and in Berlin with penicillin. But maybe that's a hook for another book:)

Big hug
Vasylysa

On polyphony of voices

From Viktoriia

Hi, Vasy,
I love the story of augmentin and penicillin. We are trying to augment the rules, because the rules failed us. Europeans are trying to neutralise the discomforts in an already comfortable space. Both are valid approaches, but ours might feel a bit too uncomfortable. I'm sorry, but not surprised you were kicked out of a discussion about peace and tolerance. I am sure this institution meant well. They want to live in a house where there is no evil, with white curtains and clean kitchen surfaces. Some muffled screams are coming from a cellar, but they were left by the previous neighbours who stored something in there. That's how the Iron Curtain worked, both ways, allowing Western Europe to build a nice wealthy society without looking in the cellar, i.e. Eastern Europe. As a Ukrainian joke goes, "The world is asking us to die more quietly."

We all speak about peace, but for Ukrainians, peace is freedom and justice — a woman with a kid in one hand and a shotgun in the other. For Europeans, peace is more abstract, a white dove and the quiet of the Western Front (a book that has been so terribly misunderstood in the recent film adaptation), and us hugging Russian artists and crying on one another's shoulders because we are so grateful to be reconciled through the wise efforts of European art institutions. Everyone sings John Lennon, and we all walk hand-in-hand into the sunset to eat marshmallows on the beach.

Europeans are wary of conflict but we Ukrainians are now made of conflict. We are a young nation that is in a constant process of re-negotiating our rules of life because we are uncomfortable with the world as it is. And I am sure that the organisers of that event in Berlin will benefit from that conflict eventually. Not that they should kick Ukrainian artists (please don't). But they saw that the picture was not that simple. And they will continue bumping into Ukrainian artists until, at some point a shift towards one another will happen. We have common values in humanness. When European leaders publicly and very resolutely supported Ukrainians after the notorious Oval Office incident, it was, I think, a shared instinct, first of all, a bodily reaction that this is not how humans should be treated.[49]

I suddenly remembered our visit to the Kharkiv Literary Museum some days after you read Shevelov at the Quiet Centre. I really liked our discussion that the city should be a conversation, a dialogue rather than a monologue. It seems to me that such simplicity opens a deeper understanding of the processes in Kharkiv. I'm not only speaking about our local government, which, of course, is always an object of discomfort,

---

49 On the 28th of February 2025 at a meeting in the Oval Office US president Trump and Vice president Vance has a verbal row with Ukrainian president Zelensky. Ukrainian society was unnerved by the incident, recognizing a familiar patterns of behavior that they had experienced before from larger states. It was particularly telling that in the moment when the row took place, Zelensky was showing Trump photographs of the Ukrainian military after Russian captivity — the evidence of torture and malnutrition.

sometimes even well-grounded.[50] *But even taking art or street art, every time an artist starts to do a little bit too much — too many images on too many streets — people get angry. Not all, but there is always a group in Kharkiv that feels the level of democracy very acutely, as if someone had stepped on their broken foot. They immediately call out such overbearing presences. Too much of the same will not be tolerated, I feel, not after the Soviet Union and its monopolising aesthetic sameness. I like this barometer of democracy, the checks and balances, this radar of street art. It starts to work, and here you get a Wall of Discord, and then Zloy Bosch — the anonymous adversary of Hamlet, and so on to stand in the way of the sameness. Polyphony is, of course, a compromised word, very much appropriated by Bakhtin and his buddy Dostoyevsky (who, to my mind, had zero polyphony and, in fact, wrote as if he had only one character with different wigs; all his books seem the same to me actually). Anyway, reclaiming this word for us immediately, I think that this conversation of real human beings and their aesthetics is essential for the Kharkiv of Skovoroda, this ideal city that remembers all the storylines and is lit from the inside (godspeed to our biolabs and secret*

---

[50] There is a feeling that we never get to see people with exceptional taste in governing roles. I got very disappointed when my candidate at the last mayor's elections, an urban scholar, got little more than 1000 votes. We probably have to accept that out taste is also subject to negotiations though, especially in public. I've been feeling warm emotions towards all the bombed and rebuilt constructions, even such seemingly un-aesthetic as Nikolsky, for instance. Every time I look at its roof that was hit by a missile in 2022, I feel a little bit like it's my child was hurt, though of course I need to feel absolute disdain towards this obsolete golden-rimmed atrocity.

nuclear programmes, of course). That is why Mitasov's story is strangely important for Kharkiv. You can be anyone and have any kind of aesthetic taste, and you can even be a little bit mad but still have the right to exist visually in Kharkiv.

Curiously, Mitasov had different writing styles for his house, the stairs, and the street. He was aware on a very unconscious level that these were different spaces and that the street was a space for some of the clearer communications. It is as if you always brush your hair before leaving home if you live in the centre of the city. When you live in your private house somewhere by the forest, you can walk in pyjamas. But in the city, you are always painfully aware of others. Even in the later stages of schizophrenia, as in Mitasov's case, people feel this restriction by the freedom of the other. It will be crucial for Kharkiv, going forward, to preserve this polyphony. I like the story of rebuilding Dresden and Warsaw, not from the aesthetic point of view, as it feels a little bit like walking along a plastic copy of a city when you are in the centre of Dresden or Warsaw. But it is important that the citizens of these places were asked what they wanted. And they said that they wanted it like before, even if it would look unnatural. Aesthetics lost a little bit, but it was a victory for democracy. And sometimes democracy is a little bit ugly, and shabby, and lame, and slow. But it is much better to breathe and walk around a democratic city. In the same way, many people I asked in Saltivka want their ugly Soviet residential buildings to be restored. Because it is theirs, and they probably have the right. I, for once wouldn't mind installing a lift in my residential building. But I feel that my neighbours wouldn't go for it. So I'll be doomed to walk the stairs. Doomed to healthy cardio by popular vote, haha. I hope at some point Europeans will also accept our augmentin, the pushiness and anarchy we could bring to the union's diversity.

Re: On polyphony of voices

Dear both,
Thank you so much for opening the door to the discussion on the polyphony of voices. It makes me think about one more issue that has not been sitting well with me for a while now. As we are writing this book, we are three human beings born in female bodies; however, up until now, we have been referring to the authors or creators who were born in male bodies. I guess what I am trying to say, is that I hope that one of the shifts in the next round of discussions would include a more diverse experience of the city both in terms of its co-creation and cohabitation.

Hugs
Vasylysa

2013

Dear Vasylysa and Viktoriia

Do you remember the autumn of 2013, Vasylysa? I have an overwhelming amount of notes, recordings, and photos documenting your life back then in case you need refreshing. The fieldwork I did with you gives a glimpse into Kharkiv before Maidan, when pro-Russian forces in the local and national government were strong and when Russian was the most commonly spoken language in the city (I even have a few recordings of you asking Danylo, the only Ukrainian speaker in the group, to speak Russian for my sake. That would be unthinkable today but the times were different). Kharkiv had been brushed up the year prior to my arrival to look bright and shiny for the Euro Cup in 2012, but the general population, it seemed, was not invited to make their mark on the space – they weren't even invited to touch the grass in the newly renovated Gorky Park.

Below, you will find a shorter and more condensed version of my master's dissertation from the Department of Anthropology at Copenhagen University in 2015. I talk about public space, however, mainly as a vehicle to talk about time. Back then, you and your friends worked hard to live and work according to the values you wanted to see reflected in the society around you, but you felt that the past kept creeping in and kept putting up blockers for the changes to manifest. Now, to me, it seems like the past is attacking Kharkiv and Ukraine full-on with tanks, drones, and missiles.

Anyway, we can talk about all this afterwards. Here goes.

Defining the contemporary — urban space and the first Ukrainian generation

Having dragged my suitcase along the busy streets from the train station, I finally arrived at Constitution Square in the centre of Kharkiv. I looked up and took a deep, healing breath. As if I had stepped through the invisible walls of a sunlit snow globe, everything suddenly seemed much nicer here. There were no bumpy pavements, no noisy trams, no honking cars, and the peeling facades of the surrounding buildings were a fading memory. The blue glass facade of the Historical Museum was glistening in the sun like a large diamond in the middle of the bright, clean, and calm square.

The Historical Museum, Universytets'ka St, 5

It is early autumn 2013. I, a 26-year-old Danish anthropology student, had travelled to Kharkiv to spend four months on fieldwork among a small group of architecture students and interior designers in their 20s; Lesya, Sergiy, Halya, Artem, Vasylysa, and Danylo.[51] They were the organising team of Architectural Adventures (AA), a community for like-minded people that hosted events like master classes and discussion nights about architecture and city planning.

The students were all members of the first generation to grow up with no memories of the former Soviet Union. I initially chose to conduct my fieldwork with them because I wondered how they related to a city which, to me, seemed heavily influenced by the Soviet past. What did they think about the many Khrushchovkas in the suburban neighbourhoods of Kharkiv? How did they feel about the Opera House that, to me, looked like a monolithic block? And what about the statue of Lenin that was posing proudly in the very centre of the largest square in Europe? Their perspectives on Soviet architecture turned out to be much more nuanced than my initial questions assumed and much less relevant.

"That building is awful," Danylo told me when we passed the blue glass facade of the Historical Museum a few weeks after my arrival. "Glass and steel do not fit into this place. The design clashes with the other build-

---

51 All names except from Vasylysa's have been changed.

ings, and it's dishonest because the brick walls are covered up." Like other areas in Kharkiv, the square had been refashioned when Kharkiv was appointed to become a host city for the Euro Cup held in 2012. Danylo explained that the building was originally constructed of red brick, which used to be its look before it was painted yellow in 2012, "now the building is trying to look like something it's not—it's an attempt to be 'so contemporary.'" The scornful tone of his voice let me know that he did not find the attempt successful.

To me, an ignorant newcomer at the time, the building looked alright. To the architecture students, I argue, the reconstruction of the Historical Museum represented a battle, not just over aesthetic choices but over time itself. The renovation of the building with the Historical Museum anchored it, not in the future, but in the past. This piece of Kharkiv was now sidelined in a parallel dimension, cut off from the global current of time that pulsed through the rest of the world and brought nourishment for ideas and innovation with it. The students themselves thrived in the current of the contemporary world; they felt its pulse, their peers felt it, and they wanted their city to feel it, too. They wanted Kharkiv to claim a proud and strong voice in the global world.

In this chapter, I want to shine a light on the connection between place and the experience of time, exemplified above in the Historical Museum. I wish to show how space-time constellations, as an experienced fact of their life, organised the world of the architecture students and how they positioned themselves in relation to them.

The chronotope; a take on time

The notion of the chronotope (from Greek, "chronos," meaning time and "topos," meaning place) was coined by the literary theorist Mikhail Bakhtin[52] in the early to mid 19th century Soviet Union. Bakhtin used the term to describe "the intrinsic connectedness of temporal and spatial relationships that are artistically expressed in literature" (Bakhtin 1981:84), and that is "colored by emotions and values" (Bakhtin 1981:243). He argued that in every story there is an implicit chronotopic backdrop which shapes how the characters can develop and how the storyline can unfold. As anthropologist Kristina Wirtz explains: "Bakhtin applied the term to express how texts mobilise temporal, spatial, and characterological motifs and frameworks to convey differing kinds of narrative trajectories, event-structures, and points of view. [...] In each literary genre, Bakhtin suggested, the chronotope as-event-horizon conditions what kinds of stories, actions, and forms of personhood are possible (see Dick 2011; Stasch 2011)." (Wirtz 2016:347). The notion of the chronotope has since been adapted by researchers of other social sciences, however, most commonly with the focus on words being uttered, either as

---

52 Yes, Viktoriia and Vasylysa, we'll need to talk about him later.

text or verbally. I use the notion of the chronotope more flexibly and argue that spatial-temporal experiences also are mediated through aesthetics, space, and actions.

In this text, I argue for the existence of the chronotope as an empirical fact, a kind of context, that is physically present to the students in Kharkiv, much the same way as Bakhtin famously put it: "Time, as it were, thickens, takes on flesh, becomes artistically visible; likewise, space becomes charged and responsive to the movements of time, plot and history." (Bakhtin 1981:84). I want to show how time, the sense of history and the sense of the future, were experienced by architecture students as they engaged with each other and the urban environment of Kharkiv. I furthermore want to show how this experience impacted the choices they made, the possibilities they saw, and the discrepancies they encountered when their chronotopic reality was challenged.

The workshop

The majority of the material informing this chapter was generated during the meetings in AA's workshop, a 25-square-metre room located in the basement of an apartment building near one of the central metro stations in Kharkiv. In the back of the room was a sofa, in the centre a table where four people could comfortably sit, and along the exterior wall of the room was a 'library:' about 20 books in English and Russian that were lined up on two of the three windowsills. Vasylysa had brought several books from the UK, the Netherlands, and Singapore where she had been on courses as a part of her education. The third windowsill was the designated 'kitchen' where the cups, the kettle, and the coffee maker belonged.

The workshop

The workshop was sporadically used during the day by the individual members of AA if they needed a place to work in between classes. On Wednesday and Saturday evenings at seven pm, however, they all got together in the workshop to coordinate, evaluate, and discuss their events and projects. Sometimes, the meetings lasted only an hour; other times, they lasted until the last metro left at a quarter past midnight. For the six members of the organising team, the workshop was a free space, a small pocket in the city, where they could develop their ideas and their professional identities. AA as an organisation existed for a couple of years altogether.

What does "contemporary" mean?

The notion of the "contemporary" [современный] kept surfacing in my conversations with the members of AA or between them as they evaluated architectural products and practices. When I started investigating what contemporary aesthetics, according to the organising team of AA was, I got explanations similar to this description from an interior project made by Lesya and Sergiy, "Bright and spacious rooms, a minimum of decoration, maximum functionality, the use of natural materials, the absence of bulky furniture, in general — a contemporary style." When Lesya and I talked about this contemporary design, she recalled an argument made by the Russian architect Sergey Skuratov, who was famous for his contemporary constructions, "We live in a contemporary world, and we do not travel in horse carriages anymore. We are contemporary people, and that kind of [historical] interior does not appear natural to us. A contemporary background should match a contemporary person with a phone, laptop, jeans, and sneakers."

The word contemporary, however, was not only applied to style and aesthetics but also to the technical, material, and social aspects of architecture. Vasylysa made the point that contemporaneity equals quality. Artem specified his understanding of the notion by suggesting alternative words such as user-orientated or comfortable, for example, in relation to infrastructure. Lesya elaborated, "There should be toilets in cafes for people with disabilities and diaper-changing facilities for families with small kids. We don't have that—as if these people don't go to cafes. McDonald's, they have it, but it's a foreign company, where it's the norm. Here, it's not like that."

Contemporary values

Discussions among the organising team of AA about what to do and how it should be done took place regularly, lengthily, and often emotionally. Despite frustration and impatience, they seemed to have developed a set of rules and agreements about how to debate. They let each other finish speaking, but when they were interrupted, they did not hesitate, saying, "Let me finish, then you can speak." If the members disagreed on a question, they called for a vote, and the result counted as conclusive. I had a conversation with Halya about the importance of the *processes* of discussing,

> "It may seem [...] that what we are doing is nothing, but we, within our small group, are deciding on such problems that people who have known each other for many years cannot solve—like people who live in the same family even—problems like: Who is responsible for what? And we share duties.

[...] "BIG[53] is a famous team but we do not have anything like that here. We have bureaus where the main architect has had the same employees for a long time, so it looks like a team, but they do not work on equal terms. [...] We want to be doing something new, something that has not appeared here yet."

Halya found the way the members of AA discussed and reached agreements rare compared to other professional teams in Kharkiv. Halya herself worked as an architect in one of the bigger offices in the city. She dreamt of establishing her own architectural office based on a different set of values than what she experienced dominated her current workplace, along with most or all other architectural offices in the city. As her comment above suggests, one of the values she sought to promote was a flat organisational structure where little is dictated by management. Communicating respectfully, having everyone's voices heard, committing to duties, and voting were all examples of a contemporary, professional approach to working, according to Halya.

Contemporary people

Having "travelled in different countries and seen what's new and interesting in the world," Lesya told me, was a quality of contemporary architects and people in general. Lesya elaborated by explaining that some people don't have the opportunity to travel, but they could still be interested in the contemporary world because they

---

53 Bjarke Ingels Group, an international architectural firm founded in Denmark in 2005.

could see everything on the Internet, "the interest should be there and the taste should be there—not everybody is like that," she added. "I prefer contemporary style." Lesya concluded her sentence thereby including herself in the group of people who have a contemporary outlook on life. When I asked Danylo if he also thought of himself as being contemporary, he answered with surprise, "All of us in AA are contemporary people! Of course!"

To the organising team of AA, the word contemporary referred to a set of values that were reflected in aesthetics and behaviour. To them, minimalism, quality of materials, good work ethics, and keeping the user's needs at the forefront were all attributes of contemporary architectural practices and aesthetics. Staying updated on global trends and ensuring democratic processes in the workplace were furthermore values inhibited by contemporary people like themselves. The organising team of AA did not experience contemporary aesthetics and values as being particularly prominent in Kharkiv. When they were hired to do interior design, for example, they were often asked to do "classical design," a task they did not have the privilege to refuse.

Soviet subjectivities with outdated preferences

"All architects cry when they are asked to do 'classical design.'" These words were uttered by the young architect, Katya, who introduced me to AA in the first place.

Katya worked as an interior designer at the time, and she pointed out some 'classical'[54] details in the café where we had met; the golden shades on the walls and sofa, the chandelier, and an imitation of a Greek column. Katya's prediction of a general aversion against 'classical style' proved to be consistent among the organising team of AA as well. Here follows a conversation with Halya about it.

"My clients are mentally disorientated; they don't know what's good for them." Halya sighed in exhaustion as she told me about her day when we met up after work. She had just spoken to a client who wanted to place a human-sized crystal figure on the dining room floor in a home of a family with young kids. "They can't tell the difference between things and style—they just think that the more expensive, the better." When I asked her why, she elaborated,

> "Ninety per cent of people who lived in the Soviet Union lived the same way; they had the same apartments, and they had the same furniture. [W]hen they were celebrating something or went on holiday they visited places like museums and theatres. These places were all constructed in the style called 'classicism'. There was a lot of gold, there were columns, and tall ceilings. I sometimes have the feeling that they associate this feeling of celebration and the sense that something is beautiful with the places of holidays from their child-

---

54 'Classical style' [Классический стиль] is not the same as 'classicism' but an interior design that evokes the sense of luxury and wealth by using pompous furniture and decorations.

hood. That's why, to them, the constructions of contemporary style seem cold and not comfortable. They don't have the experience of living in such [contemporary] spaces[55] but they do have the experience of living in golden spaces, and that's a positive one."

To Halya, a fundamental difference between herself and her clients is the source of inspiration feeding their tastes. The explanation of her client's abnormal preferences was to be found in the past, according to Halya. The contrast between the plain homes and the golden places of celebration must be feeding their choices today, she thought. By describing the mental orientation of her clients as a result of the ideals of Soviet times, she defines them as subjectivities of the past, Soviet space who had not adapted their aesthetic preferences to their lifestyle. That discrepancy made them disorientated in today's modern world.

Like Halya, Lesya linked taste to age, "For parents and elderly people here it is more difficult to accept contemporary technology and outlook on life [...] For them it's not good, they don't like it, because [to them] design and correct architecture are 'classical' homes and 'classical' things."

---

[55] Halya literally said, "they do not have the experience of living through these spaces" ("u nikh net opyta perezhivaniya prostranstva") which can be understood in a more embodied and experiential way than what is expressed in my English translation.

To the organising team of AA, 'classical style' was an aesthetic preference by people who were not contemporary, people who were shaped by the Soviet past and who were not able to adapt to modern reality. As I will show below, such Soviet subjectivities inhabited other characteristics and values as well.

Our people are strange

All the members of AA were present in the workshop along with two visiting students and a practising architect in his early thirties named Maxim. In the excerpt below, Artem, Maxim, Vasylysa, and Danylo are speaking. Artem: "Some say that our people are strange, and they say that it is a part of their [our people's] mentality to shit in the environment where they live." Artem was interrupted by Vasylysa with a reprimand about his choice of words — Artem continued, "To me, our people are strange, but it's the environment that makes us so." "I agree," Vasylysa said. "But who created such an environment?" Maxim asked. "Yes, who created it? Neighbours?" A student suggested ironically. "It's not that somebody created it," Vasylysa replied without acknowledging the joke but was interrupted by Maxim, "Let's say parents have littered, and their children are now growing in all of that" — "Not just parents" Artem interrupted, "also grandfathers and grandmothers."

Vasylysa shared her reflections from her master's project that she was currently working on, "When you have a catastrophe and no resources [in a country ruled by totalitarianism], you have to ban people from initiative and ideas, so they don't think that it can be any different. The country just doesn't have the physical resources to provide people with what they want. And that's what the Soviet Union did. But when the period of the catastrophe is over, people need to be given back the opportunity of self-realisation, but what happened was what you said [Artem]: if a person has been living in shit long enough, he will believe that that's what he deserves. We have been living in this reality for a couple decades, and it is probably the first time in this room that anyone is talking about it!" Artem began to answer, "Maybe within a generation…" but he was interrupted by Vasylysa, "Kids from our generation don't think about it!" she said as she sighed and shook her head. Danylo concluded, "We can start at least."

In this conversation, the members of AA and their peers located a perceived negligence of their fellow citizens as a personality trait of Soviet subjectivities. Vasylysa argued that the Soviet leadership discouraged people from demanding a better environment because the state was not able to accommodate their wishes. This created a generation of citizens without the desire to improve the public space around them, Vasylysa concluded.

Vasylysa's comment that the very conversation in the workshop was "the first time" anyone spoke about the problem reflected her sense of being at the beginning of a transition to a new reality. This reality was radically different from the Soviet times and from the decades that followed. Artem suggested that the new reality might be more prominent in one generation. Danylo stated that the members of AA were in a position to promote and further the transition. Despite the nuances in how they perceived the current time, the architecture students shared the view that a transition was underway and change would eventually happen, even though, as Vasylysa mentioned, some young people still grew up with old-school mindsets.

Vasylysa and Danylo were more vocal about their frustration with the experience of being between periods than their peers in AA. This is exemplified in a conversation between the two of them in the workshop one evening: "It's funny," Danylo said, "Vasylysa and I, we are the same age as Ukraine, 22 years old. It is really funny because older people, to us, they came from abroad, they are from the Soviet Union. They are not from Ukraine. They have been in Ukraine for a short period of their lives. And we want to tell them: It's our country. It's Ukraine. It's not the Soviet Union. But they're feeling like it's their land. And [they say] 'this was the Soviet Union, OK, you may call it Ukraine now, but it's our land; we made all this and —'" Vasylysa completed Danylo's sentence, " — and we still have our old values. We are working on the factories, blah, blah, blah." She interrupted herself and her imaginary narrator by exclaiming, "Shit! Come on! It's not true!"

I argue that the members of AA and their peers, as they navigated in the city and interacted with others within the field of architecture and design, experienced an intrinsic connectedness of time and space and that this experience, to them, was characterised by two coexisting sets of values: the "contemporary" and the "past/Soviet-born." I call these sets of values "chronotopes" in the Bakhtinian sense, and I understand them as "temporal and spatial relationships" that are intrinsically connected and coloured by emotions and values. The two sets of values were a backdrop of their experience as individuals, as students, and as professionals that informed their dreams for the future and their actions in the present.

To explore this further, I will in the following compare this chronotopic take to the way Deanna Davidson uses the same notion in her study of a lingering East German identity decades after the reunification of Germany.

Here: yet

Deanne Davidson conducted her research in Berlin in the early 2000s, a bit more than a decade after the reunification of Germany in 1990. Davidson shows how former East Germany, GDR, was continuously referred to as if it still existed and how inhabitants of former East Germany kept identifying as such despite the dissolution of the state. When the inhabitants of the former GDR used the words "here" (as opposed to "over there on the other side of the wall") and "back then," they situated themselves in an immediate place and a past time, which, Davidson argues, is a chronotope (Davidson 2007:213). The architecture students, I argue, did something similar but the opposite.

An important difference between our two studies is that the people Davison spoke to were older and had all lived a significant part of their lives during the GDR. It was a period they remembered fondly. Davidson explains how the narrative of former Western Germany became the official and dominating narrative for the newly unified country, "The 'here and now' of national politics, official histories, and mainstream news is a time of wealth and freedoms, a point of progress beyond fascism and dictatorship" (Davidson 2007:215). However, the "time of wealth and freedoms" was experienced by the inhabitants of former East Germany as a time of "financial insecurity, superficiality, and alienation" (Davidson 2007:216), which was a stark contrast to the values they associated with 'GDR times,' "...a period of solidarity, security, and rich intellectual and cultural life" (Davidson 2007:215).

As I showed above, the architecture students did not think of the late Soviet period and the following decades of independence as being a particularly positive chapter in the history of Ukraine. To them, the decades before and after 1991 were associated with negligence and the 1990s, in particular, were associated with violence, corruption, and "mess." As Danylo put it one evening in the workshop, "We were born in the mess between some big periods, and we don't know why the mess started or how and when it is going to end." Vasylysa added, "I'm pretty sure that when we are old, this period will be a part of history lessons in school. Our kids will be told, 'Oh, there was the period of the 90s, you know, where there were crazy guys in red jackets with golden necklaces, and they were killing each other.'" Danylo added with a narrator's voice, "It was just a little period; maybe it lasted for about twenty years." He paused but continued with a smile, "Or thirty or forty, but it was just a part of history."

Danylo and Vasylysa's description of the 1990s reflects the difficult circumstances of the country. Following the disintegration of the Soviet Union, Ukraine faced a decade of hyperinflation and poverty; the population fell from 52 million in 1989 to 48.5 million in 2001. People left the country en masse, seeking better lives in Western Europe, North America, and Israel (Yekelchyk 2007:198). There was no revolution when Ukraine went from being a republic of the Soviet Union to an independent country, and there were no clear-cut victors or obvious regime changes. Instead, many of the same politicians and industrial managers who had built socialism stayed in their positions (Yekelchyk 2007:193). Privatisation of the large public sector was implemented as a major economic policy in the 1990s. The small segment of businesspeople and politicians who understood how and were able to utilise privatisation for personal gain —

oil traders, government officials, and private businesspeople—became the new economic elite in Ukraine (Yekelchyk 2007:198).

Where the former Easteners in Davidson's study embraced the past with pride and situated themselves within it, the architecture students distanced themselves from the past. Instead, they identified with and situated themselves within the contemporary, global world. When Halya, as I quoted above, said, "We want to be doing something new, something that has not appeared here yet," she and her colleagues in AA were calling upon a present reality elsewhere, situating themselves as advocates and promoters of that present reality, that contemporary chronotope, locally in Kharkiv. To the architecture students, the contemporary chronotope was the unchallenged status quo elsewhere; it was the "real" reality and the status quo that ought to be in Kharkiv. However, because Kharkiv to them was dominated by the chronotope of the past, the contemporary chronotope was only available in patches. The Historical Museum could have been such a patch had it been renovated in the right way, but instead, it became a reincarnation of the past, right there, in the centre of the city, sparkling like a diamond.

The Historical Museum Part 2

According to an interview with the responsible architect in a local newspaper, the reconstruction of the Historical

Museum was a solution "in the spirit of the XXI century" (Zozulya 2011). A conscious decision had been made to remove the red colours of the building and the tiles on the square as a symbolic gesture indicating the shift away from the Soviet past to a European future (Zozulya 2011). The architect furthermore underlined that "In the world there are many examples of such architectural solutions," naming the Louvre in Paris and the Museum of Art in Stuttgart.

When Danylo told me that the building was awful, as I quoted him saying at the beginning of this chapter, he echoed a frustration and an opinion that had been discussed in some circles in Kharkiv since the reconstruction project became publicly known in 2011. One of the main points of contention was the yellow paint that had transformed the look of the building. The building was constructed in 1908 in dark terracotta brick in elaborate patterns with deliberate details and nuances. When the reconstruction architect and the municipality argued that they painted the brick yellow to show a shift away from the Soviet past, they failed to mention that the red colour of the brick building was not intended as a Soviet symbol at the time of its construction. The brickwork, on the other hand, was a renowned example of a particular architectural style by Borys Kornienko, one of the prominent architects in Kharkiv at the time (Rosenfeld 2024:68). This was obscured by the yellow paint.

Another point of contention concerned the blue glass facade itself. The new facade was an attempt to turn the building 180 degrees in order for the entrance to face the main square. Originally, the building had been a part of a larger complex, and it was designed with the main entrance facing away from what is the main square today. The surrounding buildings had been destroyed in WWII. In a blog post, an architect and illustrator drew the resemblance of the blue glass facade to that of the inner yard of the Jewish Museum in Berlin by the renowned architect Daniel Libeskind. She asked a question which Vasylysa picked up in her own blog post later, here paraphrased by me: Why is it necessary to copy a famous construction in Berlin? Why not come up with our own work that originates in Kharkiv, does justice to our history and reflects our identity? (Grebennik 2011).

To explore this question, I will briefly introduce the work of two other anthropologists. Alexei Yurchak shows in his analysis of the last Soviet generation (Yurchak 1997, 2006) how political usage of symbols without substance was a phenomenon characteristic of the Soviet leadership. Traditional Soviet ideology, he argues, ceased being a system of concepts and ideas which represented reality in a believable way for the last Soviet generation. This generation was related to the system of representation on the basis of pretence — they behaved as if they took the ideological messages at face value without needing to believe or disbelieve them (Yurchak 1997:185-6). Yurchak calls the representational practices of the late Soviet state "hegemony of form" (Yurchak 2006:283).

Anthropologist Elizabeth Peacock (2011) observed a similar tendency in Lviv in 2011, however, without referring to Yurchack's study. Peacock explains how a new headmaster of a public school had decided to introduce school uniforms in order to signal adherence to elite status as well as align the school with European private schools. To students, Peacock argues, the introduction of uniforms was associated with Soviet practices because it "can be equated with the Soviet practice of overemphasising surface-level changes without making any substantial policy reforms" (Peacock 2011:102).

Like Peacock argues it was the case for her interlocutors in Lviv, I suggest that the reconstruction of the Historical Museum to the architecture students was also associated with this Soviet practice, similar to the "hegemony of form" in Yurchark's terminology. With some simple and relatively cheap aesthetic tricks, the building was dressed in a different symbolic outfit in an attempt to make it signify belonging to the 21st-century global world. However, by covering up the original look of the building, the meaningful connection to history was removed. The building became an empty, disconnected symbol. By prioritising form over substance, like they used to do in the last Soviet generation, the reconstruction of the Historical Museum reproduced the values and logic of the past.

A teacher at the National University of Architecture and Construction told me that the architects behind the Historical Museum were chosen behind closed doors. There had been no contest where different architects could submit their suggestions, which was not considered by her or the architecture students in AA as 'normal.' "Here," Lesya once explained, "if the client has the money and the wish to build something, he simply pays an architectural firm to build for him. Abroad, it doesn't work like that—there are only contests. If a company wants to make a building, it makes a contest, and then the architectural firms bid."

The building housing the Historical Museum occupied a location in the cityscape resembling that of an icon. Sociologist Leslie Sklair defines an iconic building as a resource in the struggle for meaning and, therefore, for power (Sklair 2006:21). "The idea [of an icon] has two defining characteristics. First, it clearly means famous, at least for some constituencies; and second, [...] an architectural icon is imbued with a special meaning that is symbolic for a culture and/or a time, and that this special meaning has an aesthetic component. It is this unique combination of fame with symbolism and aesthetic quality that creates the icon." (Sklair 2006:25). The Historical Museum, as I showed above, was imbued with meaning by the municipal government, and the building did become somewhat famous—a judgement I made based on the central location of the building and the many people I saw taking pictures in front of it.

So, back to the original question: Why was the renovation of the Historical Museum so upsetting to the architecture students?

Conclusion

When I arrived in Kharkiv in the early autumn of 2013, I thought I would be speaking to the students about buildings from Kharkiv's Soviet past and possibly listening to their complaints about the Soviet legacy still being highly visible in the cityscape. We did speak some about that, but never in the same unequivocally negative terms as were used about the Historical Museum. The statue of Lenin in Freedom Square, for example, was not the nicest part of the city, according to the students, but they acknowledged that many of their fellow citizens still identified with it, so it might not be time to remove it just yet. Also, removing the statue would not change the past. What really mattered to the students was not the legacy of the past already imprinted in the urban space but the actions that were taken in the present that showed the orientation of Kharkiv in time and space. The renovation of the Historical Museum was exactly an example of such an action. Despite the intention, in the eyes of the architecture students, the building became a symbol of past logic and values because they saw the reconstruction process itself as shaped by outdated approaches. Those approaches were the lack of openness when electing the architectural firm for the job and how the design itself showed a disregard for the local context and signalled a preference for form over substance—a signature move of the late Soviet period.

Having past logic and values prominently reproduced in the very centre of Kharkiv was a blow to the students who saw the global rivers of the contemporary world diverge from their city, leaving Kharkiv on the sideline among stagnant water puddles. The students themselves, though, were taking action every day to manifest the values they wished to live by and the future they wished for their city to fully pursue. By staying updated on global trends, creating contemporary spaces, and working with each other in contemporary ways, they carved out wells and discovered springs through which the pulsing current of the *real* present would flow.

References

Bakhtin, M. (1981). *The Dialogic Imagination: Four Essays*. Translated by C. Emerson and M. Holquist. Edited by M. Holquist. Austin: University of Texas Press.

Davidson, D. (2007). "East spaces in West times: Deictic reference and political self-positioning in a post-socialist East German chronotope." *Language & Communication*, 27(3), 212-226.

Peacock, E.A. (2011). "Growing out of a postsocialist world: teenagers reconstructing identities in Western Ukraine". Unpublished PhD thesis, [UC San Diego].

Richardson, Tanya. 2008. Kaleidoscopic Odessa: History and Place in Contemporary Ukraine. University of Toronto Press.

Rosenfeld, Maxim. 2024. *Фасади – Facades: Харків – Kharkiv*. Kharkiv: АССА видавництво.

Sklair, Leslie. 2006. "Iconic architecture and capitalist globalization". *City*, 10(1), 21–47.

Wirtz, K. (2016). "The living, the dead, and the immanent: Reconstruction of experience in Cuban Santería." *Hau: Journal of Ethnographic Theory*, 6(1), 343-369.

Yekelchyk, Serhy. (2007). *Ukraine: Birth of a Modern Nation.* Oxford; New York: Oxford University Press.

Yurchak, Alexei. (1997). "The cynical reason of late socialism: power, pretense, and the anekdot". *Public Culture* 9(2): 161–88.

Websites

Grebennik, Olga. "Сами себе ЛИБЕСКИНД (ы)." Blogpost uploaded August 28, 2011. https://grebennik.livejournal.com/83086.html

Zozulya, Irina. Vecherniy Kharkov. "Исторический музей в Харькове развернут." Article published August 29, 2011. http://vecherniy.kharkov.ua/news/55414/

Coffee break

Reflections on 2013

*08.12.2024,
Berlin*

*Dear Hjørdis,
As I was reading it, I was wrestling with the desire to add comments to explain what I think of this or that, but I understood that I would be doing it from the perspective of now (2024), where I can look back at my younger self. Therefore, first of all, I would like to thank you for capturing that time. I remember myself being in fight mode for the biggest part of it. I feel that now, with age, I have grown calmer, as I understand that some things can take a lifetime, and sometimes not only one.*

 I am adding below a few thoughts that came to my mind as I was reading it:

- *The issue of the Bakhtin*
  - *This takes me back to our conversations about the fact that it would be great if more Ukrainian scientific works would be available in the international community so that when researchers work in a Ukrainian context could reference Ukrainian scientists.*
  - *I liked the way you linked Chronotope to East Berlin during your conference "Kharkiv under Fire" presentation in Berlin this October and now in the chapter. Personally, I feel it connects for me two*

cities that are my home in one time-space-continuum :) But that is more of the personal story, I guess.

- The furnishing of the AA room: when I saw the photo, I smiled. I hadn't remembered that the green cupboard from my childhood room was also there. And the memory of the kitchen window took me to the warm moments on the sofa with the tea. Thank you for the opportunity to jump into this memory. This morning, I read in Bohdan's Instagram his thoughts on memories as a warm blanket under which you can slide. When I first read it, I felt sad because, for me, some of the memories are still hard to visit, but this one I got to experience just now felt truly like a warm blanket, and as if we were again sitting on that sofa together.
- The conversations on interior design triggered the desire to continue this topic :) As you know, I am a big romantic and empath, and I have a hard time being critical of people's taste because I understand that it comes from many factors. One of them is – it is hard to do minimalism inside a large housing estate block – and it reminded me of the sketch I made of all the different interiors, but inside the big shelf (I think now, my green cupboard is the funny element on the photo too because it's clearly out of context). Feeling again, like talking with you all on the sofa that is also an art piece, because I remember how we wanted a modern sofa, but we didn't have money, so we covered this one with a blanket that we thought was more or less acceptable hahaha.

- *I think, sometimes, it can be hard to see changes being inside them, because one always sees the way how to improve. I guess this is what true love is — continue repairing (as one of Berlin's rubbish bins says — here again — I know you will smile because bins play an important part in Kharkiv's myth while connecting it with a global city, such as Paris (where the design, but in a different colour came from)).*
- *Our people are strange — I immediately have the song "People Are Strange" by the Doors in my head. Somehow, it was the song we listened to when I was 16 and now, I see youth of this age again listening to it over and over. Some things stay the same, and I like that, as it allows me to feel grounded, especially in these turbulent times.*
- *The Historical Museum story. For me, personally, this story is about the process of decision-making in such significant projects for the city. I think, even then, we were strongly arguing for the fact that such projects must have an Open Call Competition approach, and well, one could say, our voices were heard, as now, the current mayor in a team with Sir Norman Foster is doing Open Call after Open Call. Which makes me stumble in my tracks again. As I have lived and worked in Berlin for the past (almost) ten years, I understand that what I was unconsciously trying to bring to Kharkiv's context was participatory planning.*
In the case of Kharkiv, the external forces constantly contest its timelines, and everyone wants a piece of the pie, so we first need to physically survive and then go back to the drafting boards. But it's not how it works.

Today, while some of us ensure our physical survival, some tackle the issue of emotional survival, and some already sharpen their pencils and propose potential visions of the future, like rebuilding the Regional Administration Building. And, I know, here I might be opening a new branch of discussion, so I'll hit pause and get some borscht in order to dive into our next round. As for me, the professional question back in 2013 and today is pretty much the same: how does one build a structure that allows and supports the active participation of citizens in the decision-making on Kharkiv's urban space? How does one ensure the polyphony of voices in the urban space and its physical manifestation? The more I think about these questions, the more I remember Mitasov's bucket of paint :)

Once again, thank you so much for the opportunity to open this box of questions. I wish that one day, we will sit around the table with some tea again and talk about new ideas and analyse the changes that did take place.

Big hugs from Berlin
Vasylsya

On Shevelov and Bahtin

Dear Hjørdis and Vasylysa
Hope the borscht was tasty, Vasylysa!
Thanks to you, Hjørdis, I was able to come back to what feels like a very ancient past but was really just 2013. So much has changed! I barely remember the city then, definitely not from the anthropological perspective. I didn't reflect much, living in Kharkiv like a wild animal in my habitat. The museum's

new facade looked pretty to me at first, but as the years went by and nobody opened it, and it had no function whatsoever, I started to get angry really, realising that we were hoaxed as Kharkiv locals, that this building was just smoke and mirrors, that nobody was really going to make us a new beautiful museum, since the glass addition never had a function and didn't work a single day. And the complete opposite was the situation with the Ave Plaza shopping centre. I have to say that initially, I didn't like the project. It felt like a random platinum tooth in the mouth of original 19th-century buildings (that was before Nikolsky shopping centre, of course, when we learnt it can be way worse, haha). But then, one day, there was an exhibition of Eco-posters 4th Block Festival, on the higher floors of Ave Plaza. I will never forget that time when I looked from a panoramic window and saw the entire historical centre. A spell-binding experience. With time, I started to understand that the building fit in there somehow. Tastes change. Or maybe I was just impressed it was Oleh Drozdov's design, and started to look for senses then (I'm so easily impressed).

Anyway, I winced when you mentioned Bakhtin. It was painful to think that we were once again looking at Kharkiv through Russian eyes. Perhaps it is biased thinking on my side. At the workshop in Berlin I was very surprised that none of the international speakers knew or read any Ukrainian philosophers who lived in Kharkiv and wrote about it. All's fine, except that the workshop was dedicated to Kharkiv.[56] I remember slowly repeating "SHE-VE-LOV" to a German professor,

---

56 "Kharkiv Under Fire: Local History in Wartime" was an international workshop organized by Berlin campus of FernUniversität in Hagen October p.24—25, 2024.

who looked at me with polite giddiness as if I was not fully in my mind and was imagining him on the spot. "Where do we find that um, "Sche-viel-loff" person's translations?" she asked. I remember exerting a short laugh. Do Ukrainians look like people who have money to translate our great theorists? Then it got to me. I am a translator in the end, it is supposed to be my job. All this led to a good amount of anger on my side (I've been growing increasingly angrier every day ever since 2014). But now I was angry at myself. That's when I translated Shevelov's essay, "The Fourth Kharkiv" into English. Very obnoxiously.[57]

This essay, "The Fourth Kharkiv," is a good example of how different our vision of time in the city feels for a local. This Kharkiv time is not linear; it swings back and forth, depending on how tight the grip of the empire on our throat is at this particular moment. "The Fourth Kharkiv" speaks about imperial violence via the body of a local who has to live through all of these regimes that mutilate this body in different ways, like Ïvga's body, who is refused access to the church by a soldier she obviously has no respect for. Ïvga is from the first Kharkiv, and if she respected any army, it would be the Cossack regimen who were the first settlers. But by her time, Cossacks were dispersed, enslaved or became slave-owners, coerced by the empire. Ïvga doesn't have an army that protects her. She is alone in this new mutilated city. But she wins in

---

57 This unauthorized translation will be available until an official good one is released: Yuri Shevelov, The Fourth Kharkiv (translated by V. Grivina), Medium, https://viktoriagrivina.medium.com/the-fourth-kharkiv-by-yurii-george-shevelov-english-translation-5aa0e7312881

the end; she gets her lover back from the Russian imperial jail by becoming friends with this new local gentry, who still have Cossack trousers hidden in their drawers and therefore feel for her. It is simply amazing that Shevelov begins with this very optimistic story of Ïvga, a village woman who gets her lover back from the jaws of the empire. Even those who switched sides still remembered the previous iteration. Kvitka himself was supposed to be an honest servant of the empire, by the way; for 20 years, he was a head of Kharkiv's gentry (we know how we get attached to our mayors, haha). And yet his empathy was with this Ïvga woman. Of course, he wrote that the "good tsar" or governor or whatever saved her and her lover and so on, but we know a tongue-in-cheek message when we see one, right? The centre of his story is a Ukrainian woman who tricked all those people into giving her the man she loves back. And she wins in this impossible situation. She literally gets the upper hand [козир] because it's her land, her home, and who knows it better than her? But of course, she is shocked at what the Russian state system did to her city.[58]

I think Shelelov is critically under-appreciated as a decolonial scholar. He felt the empire's teeth on his own skin, so

---

58 To give a short explanation, Ïvga is the main character of a short story *Козир-дівка* [An Upper-Hand Girl] by a Kharkiv writer Hrihorii Kvitka-Osnovianenko. Ïvga, a village girl from near Kharkiv is in love with Levko, a village boy. Her alcoholic brother sets Levko up, making him look like a thief, and Levko is sent to a Russian imperial prison. But Ïvga goes to the city and turns the whole machine of bureaucracy upside down to get Levko out of jail. She is successful in this, and the story ends up with a wedding, of course (where Ïvga doesn't allow all of their money to be spent, because she is good at home economics, apparently, too).

he fled, and even abroad, Russian researchers continued to persecute him, even those who were themselves refugees, like Jacobson. For Shevelov Kharkiv was only liberated in 1991. You can feel it in "The Fourth Kharkiv," written in 1948 – Shevelov preparing for real liberation one day, dissecting the current state of the city. Like we are trying to do here. Of course, for me, it is a traumatic way to think of the future that there can always be this Russian state in its variations that will always be trying to hurt Kharkiv.

It's way more pleasant to think of Skovoroda, perhaps. I'm always trying to be optimistic, like Skovoroda. He could always walk away from all the troubles and make his own Sloboda Ukraine, his dear auntie (perhaps, I just need to buy a house in a village somewhere near Babaii and buy bees or something). And you know, Skovoroda predicted that Kharkiv would become the god-chosen city. For an atheist like me, it's not that promising, of course, but I hope someday Kharkiv will become Skovoroda's city of the sun. For me, one doesn't cancel the other. Shevelov is an archaeologist of the past, while Skovoroda is a dreamer of the future. They make up a good duo of Kharkiv theorists. They show us the complexity of time, like buildings from the 19th and 21st centuries that stand next to one another. You, Hjørdis, also noticed the two generations neighbouring, and you chose to study the nascent one. A dream.

Viktoriia

COFFEE BREAK 159

The Fifth Kharkiv?

From Hjørdis

Dear Vasylysa and Viktoriia
Borscht is, by definition, tasty! Now that is out of the way, I want to thank you for translating Shevelov's "The Fourth Kharkiv," Viktoriia. I was completely taken aback by Ïvga's screams in the first paragraph when I tried to translate the original text in the browser, "What is this? Save us, Mother of God!" Ha! I thought Shevelov had broken Google Translate!

It's a true pleasure for me to read Shevelov's "The Fourth Kharkiv." First, because of his writing — his funky associations, his jumpy energy, and his emotional descriptions of the city. Second, I hadn't been able to find anyone with this perspective on the history of Kharkiv, or Ukraine for that matter, when I worked on my master's dissertation in 2014.[59] *Shevelov describes how the different epochs throughout the history of Kharkiv have impacted the worldviews of the inhabitants and thereby grouped generations according to their experiences as subjectivities at a certain time and according to the knowledge they had access to about the past. Generational differences are true in all societies, I believe, but Shevelov points to a much deeper divide, where national identity is not*

---

59 I was limited to English language literature, and I mainly looked for peer-reviewed social science papers. All of my research happened between 2013–15. At the time it did not occur to me to consider decolonial perspectives as relevant for Ukraine. Now it seems like an obvious prism to look through when studying Ukraine.

shared and where historical events (those that are known to the general population) are interpreted in completely different ways. To me, as an anthropologist, this seems like a significant aspect of the Ukrainian lived experience that, to my knowledge, differs from other European societies. Deanne Davidson's study from former East Berlin and her application of the "chronotope" offered a branch to hold on to when trying to describe it. I found a somewhat related perspective in Tanya Richardson's monograph "Kaleidoscopic Odessa," but had I known about Shevelov back then, I would have leaned on him to spell out the complex role of historical and (a)national narratives in Ukraine.

I agree with you both, Vasylysa and Viktoriia, that it would be great if the works of more Ukrainian scholars were available in English. I would like to add that more contemporary studies within social sciences in English about Ukraine by Ukrainians would be hugely helpful. The main reason would be for the narratives about Ukraine to be shaped by perspectives originating inside of Ukraine instead of being defined by outsiders trying to make sense of Ukraine within the frameworks of their own cultural contexts. My dream would be for a workshop to be held in Kharkiv with anthropologists, sociologists and historians from all over the world but with a majority of Ukrainian scholars and artists where everyone tried to speak about the same topics and in earnestly listened and wanted to understand what the others were saying. The title: What are the social and academic implications of declaring Shevelov's Fifth Kharkiv?

I understand why my references to Bakhtin and his work trigger your gag reflex, Viktoriia. He is deeply embedded in the cultural mechanisms of a violent system that can only sustain itself by suppressing, exploiting, belittling, and controlling its neighbours. Ukraine has been subjugated to this for centuries, as Shevelov describes in Fourth Kharkiv. Therefore, forgive me for evoking the B guy again. I only do it to appropriate his chronotope in a way that was never his intention and to further Ukraine's cause. Despite its tainted origin story, I believe that the notion of the chronotope contributes to an understanding of what Ukrainians have to lose in today's war.

If we consider the chronotope as an "event-horizon that conditions what kinds of stories, actions, and forms of personhood are possible," as Wirtz paraphrased Bakhtin's work, then time can be understood as a context that defines what kind of life you can live, what kind of person you can become, and what kind of opportunities you might have. When the president withdrew from the Association Agreement with the EU in 2013,[60] he deliberately turned away from the contemporary chronotope and instead leaned into past logic and values. Maidan became a battle for the right to have an attractive future and, therefore, the right to exist in freedom. The war today is about the same. It is not "just" a battle over territory; it is a battle over time. It is a battle for the right to define which values to live by, which future to imagine, and the right to un-

---

[60] Viktor Yanukovych served as president for Ukraine from 2010 to 2014. When he withdrew from signing an association agreement that would bring Ukraine and the EU closer to each other protests broke out and Maidan, the Revolution of Dignity, started.

derstand the past from that perspective rather than being consumed by the outdated, irrelevant, and destructive worldview promoted by the aggressor. To many Ukrainians, existing under such conditions means not existing at all.

> "And here we are. The Fifth Kharkiv, singing Ukrainian carols under Russian bombs in the winter of 2024(...)" — Viktoriia Grivina (in a previous chapter).

What is the Fifth Kharkiv, according to Shevelov? He doesn't say that much about it because it had not materialised when he wrote the essay in 1948. However, to Shevelov, the Fifth Kharkiv would be spiritually connected to the Third Kharkiv, which was thriving in the 1920s. Ukraine was, from an administrative point of view, a republic of the USSR at the time, and Kharkiv was the capital of that republic. However, Shevelov describes how passionate debates about Ukrainian history, culture, and aspirations were taking place in art centres and universities and how factories and institutions became Ukrainianized, "full of life and madness." "Did you declare Kharkiv the capital of Ukraine?" The generation of the Third Kharkiv asked. "Fine, we will make it that way. We will fill it with Ukrainian content." Shevelov describes this generation as youthful youths with blue transparent eyelashes who wanted to conquer Kharkiv (I love this description!). Moscow didn't like the Third Kharkiv and went to destroy it in 1933 by executing or deporting the thinkers and cultural figures of that generation. Shevelov wrote, "The third Kharkiv that was heralded so passionately and tenderly, so majestically and so humanely, with such pride and with such lyricism by

Khvylovy, was buried. No obituaries, no epitaphs. In grave silence."

The Fourth Kharkiv, which followed, was taught to think in class categories, not in national categories. Kharkiv and Ukraine as a whole became a province of the Soviet Union, and even though Kharkivites adopted Ukrainian traits, they did not know about their Ukrainian roots. Their Ukrainian identity and spirit were hidden in their subconsciousness. Oppression of the Ukrainian nation, history, and identity was a deliberate policy of the Soviet regime. Shevelov predicted that when members of the Fourth Kharkiv understood that they were Ukrainians, they would shift and turn into the Fifth Kharkiv: *"(...) a new faith will flare up in their souls. The power of the outbreak of this new faith will be directly proportional to the power of the oppression under which that faith has been crushed until now. And then an open battlefield will be presented, then nihilism and egoism, self-love, and premature senile pessimism will fly away like dry shells. Then this generation will fight, and it will have a chance to win."*

Would Shevelov agree that Ukrainians today are members of the Fifth Kharkiv? I think he would. The connection to the Third Kharkiv has been established, pride in the national identity is clear, the battlefield is understood, and the refusal to be dominated by Moscow is fuelled by a long and painfully transparent history of oppression. If the Third Kharkiv was a generation of youthful youths with blue transparent eyelashes, then the Fifth Kharkiv is a generation of youthful and determined dreamers of all ages, armed and painfully aware of what they have to lose.

Shevelov passed away in 2002. I wonder what kind of traces of the Fifth Kharkiv he saw by then. In 2004, the Orange Revolution indicated that something was changing in Ukraine, and ten years later, Maidan cemented that fact. Back in 2006, I found myself surrounded by a Ukrainian community in Denmark, mostly friends of my boyfriend at the time. They all spoke Russian, and they made self-deprecating jokes about being Ukrainian, mainly repeating the same point that they were embarrassed about their cultural background. Time passed, and the jokes got fewer. My boyfriend started speaking Ukrainian, and even his mother back in Zhytomyr eventually shifted to Ukrainian. Maidan happened, and there was no more joking, only pride. Kyiv was painted in blue and yellow and people wore vyshyvankas when they dressed up. It was incredibly inspiring to experience. Something fundamental had shifted.

Viktoriia, you said that you consider Shevelov as a researcher of the past and Skovoroda as a thinker of the future. To me, Shevelov seems chokingly contemporary, considering he wrote the Fifth Kharkiv shortly after World War ll. And conversely, maybe Skovoroda's Kharkiv is already a sun? "Blind are the eyes when the pupil is closed," he said. Kharkiv's eyes are not closed; there is no pretence, only the honest truth. "Oh, open your eyes, look at it! Thus the city of Zechariah will become the real sun!"

In any case, thank you both for introducing me to Shevelov and Skovoroda. Skovoroda, by the way, seems interestingly familiar to me. He seems to be embodying the "turn the other cheek" and "Good Samaritan" kind of protestant values I grew up with in Denmark along with a touch of

Grundtvig's[61] education philosophy. I love those values, but I also recognise that the times call for the rise and armament of the Fifth Kharkiv and Europe as a whole.

---

61 N. F. S. Grundtvig, 1783–1872, was a rebel priest who challenged the established church order and ended up having a huge influence on educational philosophy and practice in Denmark.

Postscript

On the rebuilding of Kharkiv

Dear Vasylysa and Viktoriia
I would like to sum up some of the themes you both have brought up and start a conversation about that elusive bird – the future – the dream that makes us sharpen the pencil whenever possible. In the spirit of this book, I will begin by telling you a fable of my own. It is called:

> The unregulated intersection.
> Two years after my fieldwork had ended in 2013 I found myself living in Kharkiv again. I had a job in an international electronics company with an office in Kharkiv so I moved back for another two years. Every morning and evening, I had to go through a poorly designed, unregulated intersection near the office. There was always a traffic jam at the same spot, cars were honking aggressively, and everyone had to fend for themselves as they made their way to the other side. The whole scene was wrapped in a thick blanket of exhaust. Even the kindest of my colleagues with whom I sometimes hitched a ride became aggressive and blamed the morals of his fellow citizens and society as a whole when we found ourselves engulfed in the inferno. Way to start the day.

I thought of the intersection when I read your text, Vasylysa, about physical and organisational frameworks. The frameworks and the structures have a huge impact on people's attitudes and willingness to engage with each other and take part in a project.

Back in 2013, the reconstruction of the Historical Museum on Constitution Square became a symbol of outdated processes and an outdated attitude to governance, even though the project was intended as a symbol of the future. Ideally, Kharkiv should not be full of heavily contested structures after it has been rebuilt.[62] *I guess it is never possible to make sure that every new building is appreciated equally by everyone, so I cannot help but wonder how to maximise the general satisfaction and support from the multiple voices of Kharkiv in the reconstruction of the city.*

You mentioned in your text above, Vasylysa, that it would have been better if there had been an Open Call back then for multiple architectural firms to submit their suggestions and for the general public to be involved in the process of reconstructing the Historical Museum. If you were in charge of reconstructing the Historical Museum today, how would you get all the multiple voices engaged in the process?

Another question is about aesthetics. Your colleague concluded in her blog post that the new design of the Historical Museum was probably inspired by a museum in Berlin. You both made the argument that the new look of the building should have been rooted in Kharkiv's history, in something meaningful locally, not in something beautiful in a different country. Let's say that you asked the citizens of Kharkiv about their input on the new design of the Historical Museum, and the majority replied the same way as Viktoriia mentioned they did in Dresden and Warsaw, that they would prefer it to look exactly like now, yellow with a blue glass facade. Would you accept that? It sounds a bit sad to me for the aesthetics to be compromised like that, even if the process is healthy.

---

62 Or maybe I am way off. Maybe such conflicts feed the heart and soul of Kharkiv, and I am the odd one out with my "less friction is always better" attitude.

As Viktoriia said, the city is a dialogue, not a monologue, but some buildings are more important than others as symbols of a city's values and orientation in time and space. It seems to me that someone needs to be brave and suggest a design that inspires, at least when it comes to culturally important buildings, however thankless the task is. I guess that's the difference between the disciplines of street art and activism versus architecture and construction.

Maybe it is easier to find consensus on meaningful architecture and design today compared to 2013? What do you think?

PS. Isn't there an Open Call for the reconstruction of the Regional Administration building on Freedom Square? Let's submit a proposal that encapsulates Skovoroda's free spirit, the fierceness of Shevelov's Fifth Kharkiv, and the random madness of all of Kharkiv's Mitasovs.

What comes first?

Dear Hjørdis,
I am grateful to you for opening up, again, this architectural discourse for me. Back in 2013, as today, I am thinking about the question of what comes first — societal structure or the physical one? I guess, they go hand-in-hand, but before I dive into that, I feel there is a necessity to establish a difference between the space of the street and the physical structures, or, put simply, buildings.

Streets are formed by buildings, or more so, their facades. In the space of the street, the discussion that happens through the visual elements, or street art, can be, and mostly is, anonymous (unless it's brought into the online space, as in the example of the Wall of Discord).

If we move the discussion from the street into the drawing room, then, just like buildings, voices would get faces. Both of the buildings you bring in question, the Historical Museum (2013), and the Regional State Administration Building (2024), are buildings with an additional layer to them; they are public buildings. Therefore, their aesthetics could be, in theory, a reflection, or a mirror into society.

Your suggestion for submitting a competition entry for the Regional State Administration Building is an exciting and provocative one. I spoke about it to various people. Some of them were architects, some not. The answer that seems to be coming to the surface is that it might not yet be the time for this conversation, because not all the potential participants of this discussion are present at the table.

I think, just like this book, the Regional State Administration Building is there to help us collect the questions, and there are many of them. Right now, we might be in the process of identifying them. This process seems to be an important one, as I see questions as doors to new, unexpected possibilities, so allow me to note down a set of potential doors I have in my notebooks.

1. Thermometer of Pain

During one of the recent discussions, I got to attend in Kharkiv in person, Serhiy Zhadan raised the question of the growing gap between each of us due to the different levels of pain. What he meant was that not each of us had a chance to be present in that room (by coincidence close to the Regional State Administration Building) on that night, because, some of us were at the front lines, some in the medical van, some in the evacuation van, some under occupation, some scattered around the country and world, and some are watching us from the sky. How does one stitch together these different unique experiences and offer a shape for them that would be empathic, ensuring that each experience is seen and represented? This is a question I keep asking myself each day, and each time I do, I come to think that it is not even the beginning of the list of questions, or, say, requirements for the competition. The question would also be, who is forming the requirements for it. But even that, might not yet be the point for the discussion, as most of us in the past years have been working multiple jobs while dealing with growing mental exhaustion caused by sleepless nights and other mental factors that are rarely talked about during war-time, as most of the conversations are focused on the question of physical survival, meaning: support and supply for the army personnel, medical assistance to the army and civilian populations, evacuation of the civilian population, etc.

At times, I recognise my own privilege of being able to type these words in the comfort of my Berlin apartment, while my friends and professional colleagues swapped pencils for an army rifle. Sometimes, I don't know how to deal with this. It's a difficult mental load that each of us is carrying with us every single day, even on those days when you think I am smiling at you from behind the camera. The fact that we managed to write this book, for me, personally, is already a huge dream come true.

I hope, what we managed to do here, was to outline the questions that could facilitate the discussions once the time arrived for them, while, holding our spirits up in order to be brave to start those discussions ourselves.

2. How would this plaster protect me from a missile?
I was asked by an old acquaintance of mine when I showed her my work – to heal – during our spontaneous meeting in January 2025. I felt embarrassed for a second. Plasters might have served as an emotional support symbol in the summer of 2023, but is it now? On the one hand, I think it's a conversation I would be able to return to only in the future, when, hopefully, we will be seated in Pakufuda cafe (where we were having this conversation at the time) behind Derzhprom and there will be no more air raid alarms. On the other hand, the thing with time is that it is always moving, even when we don't notice it. So, I am forced to find my own answer to this question in order to be able to generate another hypothetical future, the one that might look as naive, as my 'love-medicine' plaster in the frontline of Kharkiv.

If I were to do that, I would imagine that in Kharkiv, we are at the point where the societal request for the community centre is at its peak. Then I recalled another private conversation where I was told that even if one of us became the mayor of Kharkiv right this very moment, we would still need to face the consequences of previous decisions, where a large number of potential spaces for community centres are in the hands of the private sector. In a way, when we were talking about it, I felt that we were back to square one, as in 2013. But, again, maybe, today, the conditions are different, and the external *situation would still allow for the dream of a community centre to blossom.*

I will stop in a moment, as I am going in a loop here. Also, this time, I need to get on with my professional duties in order to be able to finance my life today. I think, this is another big subject that has always been following me: how do personal decisions and public decisions interconnect?

What I note for myself before signing off are the following thoughts:

- *Feelings manifest as objects: plasters might have been my reply to the thermometer of pain I felt in 2023.*
- *Architectural planning requires architects to come and walk the streets of the places they are designing for. Coming and walking the streets – becoming part of the community – is an essential part of the successful project.*
  Important note: due to the fear of physical safety, funding is limited for Kharkiv projects, and professionals can visit the place only on their own personal terms and funding (which I have been doing throughout these years).
- *Participation requires a framework (time, space, set of rules). We, as Kharkiv'yany need more time to understand on our own what our city is about (what we love about it, and what we want to do next). Foreigners can be part of this process, but on equal terms, and not with the colonial approach of "I know what you need."*
- *Some ideas manifest as buildings. Some not.*
  Why? Is it because building requires money and decision-making power?

3. Shall we discuss the future?

In a way, we might already be doing it, as we are typing these words here. As an architect, I do believe that the subjects raised in these final chapters can, definitely, be a good basis for a planning strategy. What I get to realise with age is that one building can't be seen without context. Whether it was a right one or a wrong one we would be able to understand only over time. Also, buildings, as such, are reflections of the complex societal processes.

The question of what comes first — physical or societal structure — is like the question of the chicken and the egg, and that is the reason it is so fascinating to think about it. What I wish for is that, we, as a society, would find the strength to maintain the polyphony of voices that is present in Kharkiv, and Ukraine, while, giving it a structure that would allow for the polyphony to blossom. I think this task, should not be designed through a competition. This process should be co-created by actors from various levels of decision-making. In one way or another, this process, too, is already happening.

In 2015, when I was going to study abroad, I wanted to learn more about the bureaucratic and financial structures behind the participatory planning practice. What I discovered is that it is as fragile in Europe, as it is in Ukraine. The conversations in Berlin and Kharkiv became echoes for me and I stopped experiencing the gap. In December 2024, most of my friends and colleagues in the artistic sector were stretched thin in their physical and mental capacities. On top of that, the sector was facing one of the biggest budget cuts in its recent history.

In 2013, when, you, Hjørdis were recording us, and when we were trying to engage with the general public through our interventions, then and now, I wished for the development of tools and the necessary framework for the involvement of the citizens in decision-making. However, as I have learned in the past ten years, this is a subject that is challenging not only in Kharkiv, but in Berlin as well. So now, compared to 2013, I am less critical about the way things unfold in the city, as I know that it's a process that involves much deeper processes in society, not only in Kharkiv, but also beyond it, as everything is interconnected in unexpected ways. And, maybe, that is one of the reasons I am now more involved in artistic practice in public spaces rather than in architecture, from its planning side. I feel that in artistic practice, there is much more space for human agency on the one hand, and on the other hand, in order to do architecture, one needs a team, and currently, the team is being dispersed around the country and the world.

During the visit to Kharkiv in 2023, and later on, I kept stumbling upon one clear reminder of change in the city – an empty chair next to me. That chair symbolises for me my friends and colleagues, who are now in the army or who were forced to move away, those who deal with the processing of what happened and those who, unfortunately, don't have a chance to do it in this life anymore.

After a deep inhale & exhale, I remind myself, that the last years have shown me that there are numerous possibilities for unexpected connections. One of them is the production of this book. As an architect, I wished for this book to come to life, as a documentation of the processes and thinking that took *place in the past ten years. As an artist, I felt this process was a meaningful one for myself. As a human, I felt a connection to you, my fellow co-authors, and therefore, not alone in front of this big shift that we are going through, not only in Kharkiv, but in the world.*

You never walk alone

Dear Hjørdis and Vasylysa,
I remember our first meeting, an online call across three countries. I was sitting at a recently opened Coffee Makers on Skovoroda street. A month before, I'd met Vasylysa and we had gone to this very place. Because it is a very photogenic spot, YouTube bloggers stormed there to film their reels about the resilient Kharkiv. Sitting there with Vasylysa and our mutual friend Tanya, we immediately bumped into a couple of Ukrainian celebrities. What Vasylysa calls the "boys club" formed the new distinctly masculine face of Kharkiv. I agree that even here in this book we didn't speak much about the male gaze on the city. Funnily, in place of this Coffee Makers, there used to be a cheap drinking place, a "nalyvaika." My entire life, day or night, a couple of men would be standing outside with tiny plastic cups. Now, it's gentrified amidst the full-scale invasion. This beautiful marble floor has been cleared and polished, and beautiful tall Art Nouveau windows let the sun pierce through the entire space of the cafe. I saw many projects and business meetings take place here; some of this book was written here, too (before they banned the laptops, haha). Many of these meetings and projects were female-based; the volunteer face of Kharkiv is to a great extent female too, and so we slowly claim these spaces that used to be very

male-dominated (though one can argue that in the old nalyvaika, it was the tremendous women bartenders who held power, judging who could get a drink and who had had one too many). So that's one side of the story.

In January 2024, Russian soldiers hit the nearby National Academy of Law. Coffee Makers lost almost all of those beau-

tiful windows. I saw their call on Instagram, encouraging people to come the next day and support the business by buying a cup of coffee. Walking there along the street that was still named after the Russian poet Alexandr Pushkin, I was feeling a knot in my stomach. I passed by community workers who were given free meals and tea by a local business, specialised equipment that was clearing debris, journalists, and an elderly couple holding hands as they passed by wide-eyed. The snow and bright sun made it all look like an alien scene; the ribs of the Academy and 20 historical landmarks had been hit the night before. A feeling of deep frustration mixed with the smell of charred wood and stone in the frosty air. For some reason, I thought I'd be the only visitor to Coffee Makers. Instead, I walked into a festival of life. OSB plates being decorated, people working at the big table, people talking everywhere, not a single empty table, light indie music in the background. Cheerful, slightly hysterical baristas. I took a coffee to take away and walked out, reassured. The community heard the call and came.

On 1 March 2025, Russian soldiers once again hit the street, now named after Skovoroda. Some of the windows, recently restored, fell out again. In the Makers' stories, I saw a DJ set and a party the owners organised to lift up the spirits after another harsh night.

Every time I am in Kharkiv, when I think I will walk alone or do something alone, it is never true; there is always a *group of people who will be psyched with the idea of doing some shenanigans together. In the same way, when Vasylysa and I came to a birthday party for Pakufuda, my friend Anton, who's a co-owner of the place, said that he could not imagine so many people would come to support their business in such difficult times. Their windows were broken after a North Korean missile attack on the Derzhprom neighbourhood (which still sounds so insane to me). Anton is now developing his publishing house for board games, which is also about community, a social thing to do.*

Speaking about the future, I think we need to draw from these experiences, from the feeling that if there is a good idea, it will be supported, and people will come. You will never walk alone. Now the question is, if businesses will come, and how to further develop our diversity, to make Kharkiv comfortable for all. For that, we will need the participation of the men and women now serving at the frontline for sure. Our mayor said in 2024 that Kharkiv will be the first accessible city in Ukraine. For that to happen, we need to count every kerb; we need to literally walk with a pushchair and drive in a wheelchair over the entire surface of the city. So it is not only about the architecture of the buildings, but our ability to widen the access to the "club." Submitting projects to Norman Forster's contest is important. But first, I think we need to make sure that the experts in Kharkiv are there on the jury, and we need to change the rules of the contest. I feel it is a debate for the future. As you said, we have one chair empty now at every table and need to wait for the others to return.

Many things start with a piece of paper

Dear Viktoriia,
Dear Hjørdis,
Today, I saw a beautiful video of a Kharkiv tram. The video depicts a regular tram that operates on a daily basis. It was decorated with beautiful heart-shaped cut-outs, angels and blinking lights—a reminder of Valentine's Day. The entry mentioned that the tram is operated by a woman, and that it might be that she is the one who took the initiative to decorate the tram. One could discuss at great length the aesthetics of the cut-out shapes or drawings on the windows, but, I think, it's already a huge win for us as a society. Why? Because we care about our spaces. Because we take the initiative. I believe, once again, this is the right of the city that seems to have been born during the last few years, and while everything can be constantly improved, changed, or discussed, sometimes, it's important to simply remind each other of what a great job we are doing here. In that spirit, I would like to say thank you & congratulations to us on going through the winter of 2024–2025 together and with Kharkiv. I wish for the set of questions we raise here to lead to new conversations, discussions and dreams. To get this ball rolling, I would like to suggest that we and our readers take a pen and paper, and write a letter to Kharkiv.

Since 24.02, I have been talking about Kharkiv in every sentence I am able to. At one point, one of my friends told me that I repeat the sentence, "By the way, I am from Kharkiv," so often, as if it's a sort of magic spell. Sometimes, I think it is, as I have felt since 2022, that the more I speak about

*Kharkiv, the bigger its fan base becomes, and, as my friend B. said **when you love something, you care for it**. That's simple.*

I remember how, in 2022, Kharkiv's independent media outlet LYUK had an Open Call Letter to Kharkiv. Those of us who were dreaming of Kharkiv's streets were typing love letters to our Unbreakable. I typed mine as well, but I would need a moment to look for it, as that time it didn't get published. But it didn't matter to me at the time. What mattered was that I saw that I was not alone. There are more of us, who close our eyes and walk Kharkiv's streets until we are able to do it physically.

*In a way, for me, this book project became a longer love letter to Kharkiv that we have been weaving together with you through our letters, calls, and heart emoji's in chats. After all our work I think, I believe even stronger, that Kharkiv is a dream. Just like Skovoroda, Kharkiv is an elusive philosopher who teaches you from the heart. It teaches you that dreams are free, dreams are full of imagination, and they allow us to create that which is not yet there, to reach beyond the limit of what we already know in order to discover something new. For me, Kharkiv is all that and even more. Kharkiv is a complex city, and there are many things one could argue about, but what matters to me, is that **we keep doing it—we keep walking and we keep co-creating dreams and Kharkiv's streets**.*

PS. I already imagine the next book, or magazine, as a potential participatory manifesto that would support us in the process of co-building this gorgeous city.

Dear Kharkiv

How do you fall in love with someone? Their eyes? The way they laugh? The way they make you feel? The conversations you can have with each other? The silence you can enjoy together? The way they inspire you to challenge yourself? The way they embrace all of you, including the flaws you are perfectly aware of? The dreams that you share?

That is how I feel about you, about Ukraine.

With love,
Hjørdis

Dear Xa,
Every time I return, I go and hug the coarse grey walls of Derzhprom to make sure you are both real. When the enemy is gone, I would like to lie on the cobblestones of Freedom Square and watch planes leave white traces in the wild blue sky as they fly to London, Vienna, or Istanbul. I probably won't because you never know when a crazy taxi driver decides to cut through the square diagonally, haha. But, in seriousness, I have a lot of plans for us both after victory, so hold on in there.

Hugs,
Viktoriia

A long time ago, a friend of mine (with whom we studied at the same school), asked me, when I miss Kharkiv what do I do (we had both been living abroad for over five years at the time)? My answer typed itself: I close my eyes, and I walk the streets of Kharkiv.

Usually, my route starts at the Yaroslava Mudroho Metro Station and goes down to the Historical Museum (where you would discover the Historical Museum from Hjørdis's, as well as the thermometer from the book cover, dear reader). Since 2023, my walk stayed the same, only with a twist — now I usually walked backwards from the Historical Museum towards Yaroslava Mudroho, or, as in 2024, towards the Regional State Administration Building, and then to the Quiet Center Residency behind Derzhprom. These stories are complex and might not always be clear, but they write themselves, because they come from the heart. I think that is what Skovoroda was trying to tell us, when he spoke about cardiophilosophy — one needs to walk the streets and participate in their life, either by walking, or, also, by creating. Whenever I miss my Home, I walk in my dreams, but in reality, I look for ways to build cultural bridges between Kharkiv and the place I am at, because I choose to be Kharkiv'yanka, as I do feel, my heart has been forged by these streets and I want to be part of them. See you soon, my dear.

Love,
Vasylysa

PS. Dear Reader, if you would like to share your thoughts, ideas, projects for the next Kharkiv dreams and dreams for

Postscript

Kharkiv, or connections that you would like to establish, feel free to reach out to us under:

Email kharkivisadream@gmail.com
Instagram @kharkivisadream
Twitter (X): @kharkivisadream
Bluesky: @kharkivisadream.bsky.social

Thank you notes

Hjørdis: I am grateful to everyone who welcomed me in Kharkiv, and to all those I had the privilege of meeting during my fieldwork—especially the six members of AA. Thank you for so generously sharing your time, your honest thoughts, and your lived experiences with me. Your patience, kindness, and trust made both my fieldwork and this book possible.

Viktoriia: I want to thank my family, my loved ones and friends for being there with me in this strange life. As well as to all the Kharkivians who spread the religion of Kharkiv's awesomeness across the world.

Vasylysa: I am grateful to my parents, my teachers (artist & graphic designer Iryna Alexandrova and artist, poster artist, and graphic designer Vitaly Kulikov), my friends, strangers, and everyone who has been guiding me through life and teaching me how to find the next step.

Visual Diary

Kharkiv in 2013, as seen by Hjørdis

Kharkiv in 2018 - 2025, as seen by Viktoriia

Kharkiv in 2023 - 2025, as seen by Vasylysa

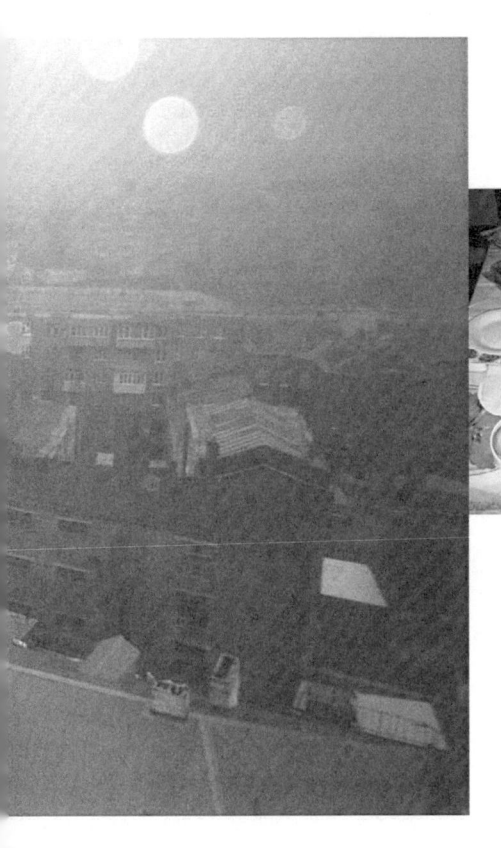

UKRAINIAN VOICES

Collected by Andreas Umland

1 Mychailo Wynnyckyj
   Ukraine's Maidan, Russia's War
   A Chronicle and Analysis of the Revolution of Dignity
   With a foreword by Serhii Plokhy
   ISBN 978-3-8382-1327-9

2 Olexander Hryb
   Understanding Contemporary Ukrainian and Russian Nationalism
   The Post-Soviet Cossack Revival and Ukraine's National Security
   With a foreword by Vitali Vitaliev
   ISBN 978-3-8382-1377-4

3 Marko Bojcun
   Towards a Political Economy of Ukraine
   Selected Essays 1990–2015
   With a foreword by John-Paul Himka
   ISBN 978-3-8382-1368-2

4 Volodymyr Yermolenko (ed.)
   Ukraine in Histories and Stories
   Essays by Ukrainian Intellectuals
   With a preface by Peter Pomerantsev
   ISBN 978-3-8382-1456-6

5 Mykola Riabchuk
   At the Fence of Metternich's Garden
   Essays on Europe, Ukraine, and Europeanization
   ISBN 978-3-8382-1484-9

6 Marta Dyczok
   Ukraine Calling
   A Kaleidoscope from Hromadske Radio 2016–2019
   With a foreword by Andriy Kulykov
   ISBN 978-3-8382-1472-6

7 Olexander Scherba
   Ukraine vs. Darkness
   Undiplomatic Thoughts
   With a foreword by Adrian Karatnycky
   ISBN 978-3-8382-1501-3

8 Olesya Yaremchuk
   Our Others
   Stories of Ukrainian Diversity
   With a foreword by Ostap Slyvynsky
   Translated from the Ukrainian by Zenia Tompkins and Hanna Leliv
   ISBN 978-3-8382-1475-7

9 Nataliya Gumenyuk
   Die verlorene Insel
   Geschichten von der besetzten Krim
   Mit einem Vorwort von Alice Bota
   Aus dem Ukrainischen übersetzt von Johann Zajaczkowski
   ISBN 978-3-8382-1499-3

10 Olena Stiazhkina
   Zero Point Ukraine
   Four Essays on World War II
   Translated from the Ukrainian by Svitlana Kulinska
   ISBN 978-3-8382-1550-1

11 Oleksii Sinchenko, Dmytro Stus, Leonid Finberg (compilers)
    Ukrainian Dissidents
    An Anthology of Texts
    ISBN 978-3-8382-1551-8

12 John-Paul Himka
    Ukrainian Nationalists and the Holocaust
    OUN and UPA's Participation in the Destruction of Ukrainian Jewry, 1941–1944
    ISBN 978-3-8382-1548-8

13 Andrey Demartino
    False Mirrors
    The Weaponization of Social Media in Russia's Operation to Annex Crimea
    With a foreword by Oleksiy Danilov
    ISBN 978-3-8382-1533-4

14 Svitlana Biedarieva (ed.)
    Contemporary Ukrainian and Baltic Art
    Political and Social Perspectives, 1991–2021
    ISBN 978-3-8382-1526-6

15 Olesya Khromeychuk
    A Loss
    The Story of a Dead Soldier Told by His Sister
    With a foreword by Andrey Kurkov
    ISBN 978-3-8382-1570-9

16 Marieluise Beck (Hg.)
    Ukraine verstehen
    Auf den Spuren von Terror und Gewalt
    Mit einem Vorwort von Dmytro Kuleba
    ISBN 978-3-8382-1653-9

17 Stanislav Aseyev
    Heller Weg
    Geschichte eines Konzentrationslagers im Donbass 2017–2019
    Aus dem Russischen übersetzt von Martina Steis und Charis Haska
    ISBN 978-3-8382-1620-1

18 Mykola Davydiuk
    Wie funktioniert Putins Propaganda?
    Anmerkungen zum Informationskrieg des Kremls
    Aus dem Ukrainischen übersetzt von Christian Weise
    ISBN 978-3-8382-1628-7

19 Olesya Yaremchuk
    Unsere Anderen
    Geschichten ukrainischer Vielfalt
    Aus dem Ukrainischen übersetzt von Christian Weise
    ISBN 978-3-8382-1635-5

20 Oleksandr Mykhed
    „Dein Blut wird die Kohle tränken"
    Über die Ostukraine
    Aus dem Ukrainischen übersetzt von Simon Muschick und Dario Planert
    ISBN 978-3-8382-1648-5

21 Vakhtang Kipiani (Hg.)
    Der Zweite Weltkrieg in der Ukraine
    Geschichte und Lebensgeschichten
    Aus dem Ukrainischen übersetzt von Margarita Grinko
    ISBN 978-3-8382-1622-5

22 Vakhtang Kipiani (ed.)
    World War II, Uncontrived and Unredacted
    Testimonies from Ukraine
    Translated from the Ukrainian by Zenia Tompkins and Daisy Gibbons
    ISBN 978-3-8382-1621-8

23 **Dmytro Stus**
Vasyl Stus
Life in Creativity
Translated from the Ukrainian by
Ludmila Bachurina
ISBN 978-3-8382-1631-7

24 **Vitalii Ogiienko (ed.)**
The Holodomor and the
Origins of the Soviet Man
Reading the Testimony of
Anastasia Lysyvets
With forewords by Natalka
Bilotserkivets and Serhy
Yekelchyk
Translated from the Ukrainian by
Alla Parkhomenko and
Alexander J. Motyl
ISBN 978-3-8382-1616-4

25 **Vladislav Davidzon**
Jewish-Ukrainian Relations
and the Birth of a Political
Nation
Selected Writings 2013-2021
With a foreword by Bernard-
Henri Lévy
ISBN 978-3-8382-1509-9

26 **Serhy Yekelchyk**
Writing the Nation
The Ukrainian Historical
Profession in Independent
Ukraine and the Diaspora
ISBN 978-3-8382-1695-9

27 **Ildi Eperjesi, Oleksandr Kachura**
Shreds of War
Fates from the Donbas Frontline
2014-2019
With a foreword by Olexiy
Haran
ISBN 978-3-8382-1680-5

28 **Oleksandr Melnyk**
World War II as an Identity
Project
Historicism, Legitimacy
Contests, and the (Re-)Construction of Political Communities in Ukraine, 1939–1946
With a foreword by David R.
Marples
ISBN 978-3-8382-1704-8

29 **Olesya Khromeychuk**
Ein Verlust
Die Geschichte eines gefallenen
ukrainischen Soldaten, erzählt
von seiner Schwester
Mit einem Vorwort von Andrej
Kurkow
Aus dem Englischen übersetzt
von Lily Sophie
ISBN 978-3-8382-1770-3

30 **Tamara Martsenyuk, Tetiana Kostiuchenko (eds.)**
Russia's War in Ukraine
During 2022
Personal Experiences of
Ukrainian Scholars
ISBN 978-3-8382-1757-4

31 **Ildikó Eperjesi, Oleksandr Kachura**
Shreds of War. Vol. 2
Fates from Crimea 2015–2022
With an interview of Oleh
Sentsov
ISBN 978-3-8382-1780-2

32 **Yuriy Lukanov**
The Press
How Russia Destroyed Media
Freedom in Crimea
With a foreword by Taras Kuzio
ISBN 978-3-8382-1784-0

33 **Megan Buskey**
Ukraine Is Not Dead Yet
A Family Story of Exile and
Return
ISBN 978-3-8382-1691-1

34 Vira Ageyeva
Behind the Scenes of the Empire
Essays on Cultural Relationships between Ukraine and Russia
With a foreword by Oksana Zabuzhko
ISBN 978-3-8382-1748-2

35 Marieluise Beck (ed.)
Understanding Ukraine
Tracing the Roots of Terror and Violence
With a foreword by Dmytro Kuleba
ISBN 978-3-8382-1773-4

36 Olesya Khromeychuk
A Loss
The Story of a Dead Soldier Told by His Sister, 2nd edn.
With a foreword by Philippe Sands
With a preface by Andrii Kurkov
ISBN 978-3-8382-1870-0

37 Taras Kuzio, Stefan Jajecznyk-Kelman
Fascism and Genocide
Russia's War Against Ukrainians
ISBN 978-3-8382-1791-8

38 Alina Nychyk
Ukraine Vis-à-Vis Russia and the EU
Misperceptions of Foreign Challenges in Times of War, 2014–2015
With a foreword by Paul D'Anieri
ISBN 978-3-8382-1767-3

39 Sasha Dovzhyk (ed.)
Ukraine Lab
Global Security, Environment, and Disinformation Through the Prism of Ukraine
With a foreword by Rory Finnin
ISBN 978-3-8382-1805-2

40 Serhiy Kvit
Media, History, and Education
Three Ways to Ukrainian Independence
With a preface by Diane Francis
ISBN 978-3-8382-1807-6

41 Anna Romandash
Women of Ukraine
Reportages from the War and Beyond
ISBN 978-3-8382-1819-9

42 Dominika Rank
Matzewe in meinem Garten
Abenteuer eines jüdischen Heritage-Touristen in der Ukraine
ISBN 978-3-8382-1810-6

43 Myroslaw Marynowytsch
Das Universum hinter dem Stacheldraht
Memoiren eines sowjet-ukrainischen Dissidenten
Mit einem Vorwort von Timothy Snyder und einem Nachwort von Max Hartmann
ISBN 978-3-8382-1806-9

44 Konstantin Sigow
Für Deine und meine Freiheit
Europäische Revolutions- und Kriegserfahrungen im heutigen Kyjiw
Mit einem Vorwort von Karl Schlögel
Herausgegeben von Regula M. Zwahlen
ISBN 978-3-8382-1755-0

45 Kateryna Pylypchuk
The War that Changed Us
Ukrainian Novellas, Poems, and Essays from 2022
With a foreword by Victor Yushchenko
Paperback
ISBN 978-3-8382-1859-5
Hardcover
ISBN 978-3-8382-1860-1

46 *Kyrylo Tkachenko*
Rechte Tür Links
Radikale Linke in Deutschland, die Revolution und der Krieg in der Ukraine, 2013-2018
ISBN 978-3-8382-1711-6

47 *Alexander Strashny*
The Ukrainian Mentality
An Ethno-Psychological, Historical and Comparative Exploration
With a foreword by Antonina Lovochkina
Translated from the Ukrainian by Michael M. Naydan and Olha Tytarenko
ISBN 978-3-8382-1886-1

48 *Alona Shestopalova*
From Screens to Battlefields
Tracing the Construction of Enemies on Russian Television
With a foreword by Nina Jankowicz
ISBN 978-3-8382-1884-7

49 *Iaroslav Petik*
Politics and Society in the Ukrainian People's Republic (1917–1921) and Contemporary Ukraine (2013–2022)
A Comparative Analysis
With a foreword by Mykola Doroshko
ISBN 978-3-8382-1817-5

50 *Serhii Plokhy*
Der Mann mit der Giftpistole
Eine Spionageschichte aus dem Kalten Krieg
ISBN 978-3-8382-1789-5

51 *Vakhtang Kipiani*
Ukrainische Dissidenten unter der Sowjetmacht
Im Kampf um Wahrheit und Freiheit
Aus dem Ukrainischen übersetzt von Christian Weise
ISBN 978-3-8382-1890-8

52 *Dmytro Shestakov*
When Businesses Test Hypotheses
A Four-Step Approach to Risk Management for Innovative Startups
With a foreword by Anthony J. Tether
ISBN 978-3-8382-1883-0

53 *Larissa Babij*
A Kind of Refugee
The Story of an American Who Refused to Leave Ukraine
With a foreword by Vladislav Davidzon
ISBN 978-3-8382-1898-4

54 *Julia Davis*
In Their Own Words
How Russian Propagandists Reveal Putin's Intentions
With a foreword by Timothy Snyder
ISBN 978-3-8382-1909-7

55 *Sonya Atlantova, Oleksandr Klymenko*
Icons on Ammo Boxes
Painting Life on the Remnants of Russia's War in Donbas, 2014-21
Translated from the Ukrainian by Anastasya Knyazhytska
ISBN 978-3-8382-1892-2

56 *Leonid Ushkalov*
Catching an Elusive Bird
The Life of Hryhorii Skovoroda
Translated from the Ukrainian by Natalia Komarova
ISBN 978-3-8382-1894-6

57 *Vakhtang Kipiani*
Ein Land weiblichen Geschlechts
Ukrainische Frauenschicksale im 20. und 21. Jahrhundert
Aus dem Ukrainischen übersetzt von Christian Weise
ISBN 978-3-8382-1891-5

58 Petro Rychlo
„Zerrissne Saiten einer
überlauten Harfe ..."
Deutschjüdische Dichter der
Bukowina
ISBN 978-3-8382-1893-9

59 Volodymyr Paniotto
Sociology in Jokes
An Entertaining Introduction
ISBN 978-3-8382-1857-1

60 Josef Wallmannsberger
(ed.)
Executing Renaissances
The Poetological Nation of
Ukraine
ISBN 978-3-8382-1741-3

61 Pavlo Kazarin
The Wild West of Eastern
Europe
A Ukrainian Guide on Breaking
Free from Empire
Translated from the Ukrainian
by Dominique Hoffman
ISBN 978-3-8382-1842-7

62 Ernest Gyidel
Ukrainian Public
Nationalism in the General
Government
The Case of *Krakivski Visti*,
1940–1944
With a foreword by David R.
Marples
ISBN 978-3-8382-1865-6

63 Olexander Hryb
Understanding
Contemporary Russian
Militarism
From Revolutionary to New
Generation Warfare
With a foreword by Mark Laity
ISBN 978-3-8382-1927-1

64 Orysia Hrudka, Bohdan Ben
Dark Days, Determined
People
Stories from Ukraine under Siege
With a foreword by Myroslav
Marynovych
ISBN 978-3-8382-1958-5

65 Oleksandr Pankieiev (ed.)
Narratives of the Russo-
Ukrainian War
A Look Within and Without
With a foreword by Natalia
Khanenko-Friesen
ISBN 978-3-8382-1964-6

66 Roman Sohn, Ariana Gic
(eds.)
Unrecognized War
The Fight for Truth about
Russia's War on Ukraine
With a foreword by Viktor
Yushchenko
ISBN 978-3-8382-1947-9

67 Paul Robert Magocsi
Ukraina Redux
Schon wieder die Ukraine ...
ISBN 978-3-8382-1942-4

68 Paul Robert Magocsi
L'Ucraina Ritrovata
Sullo Stato e l'Identità Nazionale
ISBN 978-3-8382-1982-0

69 Max Hartmann
Ein Schrei der Verzweiflung
Aquarelle von Danylo Movchan
zu Russlands Krieg in der
Ukraine
Mit einem Vorwort von Mateusz
Sora
Paperback
ISBN 978-3-8382-2011-6
Hardcover
ISBN 978-3-8382-2012-3

70 Vakhtang Kebuladze (Hg.)
Die Zukunft, die wir uns
wünschen
Essays aus der Ukraine
ISBN 978-3-8382-1531-0

71 Marieluise Beck, Jan Claas Behrends, Gelinada Grinchenko und Oksana Mikheieva (Hgg.)
Deutsch-ukrainische Geschichten
Bruchstücke aus einer gemeinsamen Vergangenheit
ISBN 978-3-8382-2053-6

72 Pavlo Kazarin
Der Wilde Westen Ost-Europas
Der ukrainische Weg aus dem Imperium
Aus dem Ukrainischen übersetzt von Christian Weise
ISBN 978-3-8382-1843-4

73 Radomyr Mokryk
Die ukrainischen »Sechziger«
Chronologie einer Revolte
ISBN 978-3-8382-1873-1

74 Leonid Finberg
My Ukraine
Rethinking the Past, Building the Present
ISBN 978-3-8382-1974-5

75 Joseph Zissels
Consider My Inmost Thoughts
Essays, Lectures, and Interviews on Ukrainian Matters at the Turn of the Century
ISBN 978-3-8382-1975-2

76 Margarita Yehorchenko, Iryna Berlyand, Ihor Vinokurov (eds.)
Jewish Addresses in Ukraine
A Guide-Book
With a foreword by Leonid Finberg
ISB 978-3-8382-1976-9

77 Viktoriia Grivina
Kharkiv—A War City
A Collection of Essays from 2022–23
ISBN 978-3-8382-1988-2

78 Hjørdis Clemmensen, Viktoriia Grivina, Vasylysa Shchogoleva
Kharkiv Is a Dream
Public Art and Activism 2013–2023
With a foreword by Bohdan Volynskyi
ISBN 978-3-8382-2005-5

79 Olga Khomenko
The Faraway Sky of Kyiv
Ukrainians in the War
With a foreword by Hiroaki Kuromiya
ISBN 978-3-8382-2006-2

80 Daria Mattingly, Jonathon Vsetecka (eds.)
The Holodomor in Global Perspective
How the Famine in Ukraine Shaped the World
With a foreword by Anne Applebaum
ISBN 978-3-8382-1953-0

81 Olga Khomenko
Ukrainians beyond Borders
Nine Life Journeys Through the History of Eastern Europe
With a foreword by Zbigniew Wojnowski
ISBN 978-3-8382-2007-9

82 Mykhailo Minakov
From Servant to Leader
Chronicles of Ukraine under the Zelensky Presidency, 2019–2024
With a foreword by John Lloyd
ISBN 978-3-8382-2002-4

83 Volodymyr Hromov (ed.)
A Ruined Home
Sketches of War, 2022–2023
ISBN 978-3-8382-2008-6

84 Olha Tatokhina (ed.)
Why Do They Kill Our People?
Russia's War Against Ukraine as
Told by Ukrainians
With a foreword by Volodymyr
Yermolenko
ISBN 978-3-8382-2056-7

85 Mieste Hotopp-Riecke,
Sarah Reinke (Hrsg.)
Die Krimtataren
Geschichte – Kultur – Politik
Mit einem Vorwort von
Nariman Dschelal
ISBN 978-3-8382-1986-8

86 Max Hartmann (ed.)
A Cry of Despair
Danylo Movchan's Watercolors
on the War in Ukraine
With a foreword by John A.
Kohan and Matheusz Sora
ISBN 978-3-8382-2051-2

87 Olha Marmilova, Yuliia
Soroka (eds.)
The Russian War Against
Ukraine
Investigations of Its Social and
Historical Context, 2014–2024
With a foreword by Ulrich
Schmid
ISBN 978-3-8382-2035-2

88 Mykola Davidyuk
How Putin's Propaganda
Works
Ukraine's Experience in Its War
Against Russia since 2014
With a foreword by Roman
Kostenko
ISBN 978-3-8382-1627-0

89 Mikhail Minakov
Der postsowjetische Mensch
Philosophische Betrachtungen
zur Gesellschaftsgeschichte nach
Ende der UdSSR
Mit einem Vorwort von Timm
Beichelt
Aus dem Englischen übersetzt
von Hermann Haushahn
ISBN 978-3-8382-2043-7

Book series "Ukrainian Voices"

Coordinator
Andreas Umland, National University of Kyiv-Mohyla Academy

Editorial Board
Lesia Bidochko, National University of Kyiv-Mohyla Academy
Svitlana Biedarieva, George Washington University, DC, USA
Ivan Gomza, Kyiv School of Economics, Ukraine
Natalie Jaresko, Aspen Institute, Kyiv/Washington
Olena Lennon, University of New Haven, West Haven, USA
Kateryna Yushchenko, First Lady of Ukraine 2005-2010, Kyiv
Oleksandr Zabirko, University of Regensburg, Germany

Advisory Board
Iuliia Bentia, National Academy of Arts of Ukraine, Kyiv
Natalya Belitser, Pylyp Orlyk Institute for Democracy, Kyiv
Oleksandra Bienert, Humboldt University of Berlin, Germany
Sergiy Bilenky, Canadian Institute of Ukrainian Studies, Toronto
Tymofii Brik, Kyiv School of Economics, Ukraine
Olga Brusylovska, Mechnikov National University, Odesa
Mariana Budjeryn, Harvard University, Cambridge, USA
Volodymyr Bugrov, Shevchenko National University, Kyiv
Olga Burlyuk, University of Amsterdam, The Netherlands
Yevhen Bystrytsky, NAS Institute of Philosophy, Kyiv
Andrii Danylenko, Pace University, New York, USA
Vladislav Davidzon, Atlantic Council, Washington/Paris
Mykola Davydiuk, Think Tank "Polityka," Kyiv
Andrii Demartino, National Security and Defense Council, Kyiv
Vadym Denisenko, Ukrainian Institute for the Future, Kyiv
Oleksandr Donii, Center for Political Values Studies, Kyiv
Volodymyr Dubovyk, Mechnikov National University, Odesa
Volodymyr Dubrovskiy, CASE Ukraine, Kyiv
Diana Dutsyk, National University of Kyiv-Mohyla Academy
Marta Dyczok, Western University, Ontario, Canada
Yevhen Fedchenko, National University of Kyiv-Mohyla Academy
Sofiya Filonenko, State Pedagogical University of Berdyansk
Oleksandr Fisun, Karazin National University, Kharkiv
Oksana Forostyna, Webjournal "Ukraina Moderna," Kyiv
Roman Goncharenko, Broadcaster "Deutsche Welle," Bonn
George Grabowicz, Harvard University, Cambridge, USA
Gelinada Grinchenko, Karazin National University, Kharkiv
Kateryna Härtel, Federal Union of European Nationalities, Brussels
Nataliia Hendel, University of Geneva, Switzerland
Anton Herashchenko, Kyiv School of Public Administration
John-Paul Himka, University of Alberta, Edmonton
Ola Hnatiuk, National University of Kyiv-Mohyla Academy
Oleksandr Holubov, Broadcaster "Deutsche Welle," Bonn
Yaroslav Hrytsak, Ukrainian Catholic University, Lviv
Oleksandra Humenna, National University of Kyiv-Mohyla Academy
Tamara Hundorova, NAS Institute of Literature, Kyiv
Oksana Huss, University of Bologna, Italy
Oleksandra Iwaniuk, University of Warsaw, Poland
Mykola Kapitonenko, Shevchenko National University, Kyiv
Georgiy Kasianov, Marie Curie-Skłodowska University, Lublin
Vakhtang Kebuladze, Shevchenko National University, Kyiv
Natalia Khanenko-Friesen, University of Alberta, Edmonton
Victoria Khiterer, Millersville University of Pennsylvania, USA
Oksana Kis, NAS Institute of Ethnology, Lviv
Pavlo Klimkin, Center for National Resilience and Development, Kyiv
Oleksandra Kolomiiets, Center for Economic Strategy, Kyiv

Sergiy Korsunsky, Kobe Gakuin University, Japan
Nadiia Koval, Kyiv School of Economics, Ukraine
Volodymyr Kravchenko, University of Alberta, Edmonton
Oleksiy Kresin, NAS Koretskiy Institute of State and Law, Kyiv
Anatoliy Kruglashov, Fedkovych National University, Chernivtsi
Andrey Kurkov, PEN Ukraine, Kyiv
Ostap Kushnir, Lazarski University, Warsaw
Taras Kuzio, National University of Kyiv-Mohyla Academy
Serhii Kvit, National University of Kyiv-Mohyla Academy
Yuliya Ladygina, The Pennsylvania State University, USA
Yevhen Mahda, Institute of World Policy, Kyiv
Victoria Malko, California State University, Fresno, USA
Yulia Marushevska, Security and Defense Center (SAND), Kyiv
Myroslav Marynovych, Ukrainian Catholic University, Lviv
Oleksandra Matviichuk, Center for Civil Liberties, Kyiv
Mykhailo Minakov, Kennan Institute, Washington, USA
Anton Moiseienko, The Australian National University, Canberra
Alexander Motyl, Rutgers University-Newark, USA
Vlad Mykhnenko, University of Oxford, United Kingdom
Vitalii Ogiienko, Ukrainian Institute of National Remembrance, Kyiv
Olga Onuch, University of Manchester, United Kingdom
Olesya Ostrovska, Museum "Mystetskyi Arsenal," Kyiv
Anna Osypchuk, National University of Kyiv-Mohyla Academy
Oleksandr Pankieiev, University of Alberta, Edmonton
Oleksiy Panych, Publishing House "Dukh i Litera," Kyiv
Valerii Pekar, Kyiv-Mohyla Business School, Ukraine
Yohanan Petrovsky-Shtern, Northwestern University, Chicago
Serhii Plokhy, Harvard University, Cambridge, USA
Andrii Portnov, Viadrina University, Frankfurt-Oder, Germany
Maryna Rabinovych, Kyiv School of Economics, Ukraine
Valentyna Romanova, Institute of Developing Economies, Tokyo
Natalya Ryabinska, Collegium Civitas, Warsaw, Poland
Darya Tsymbalyk, University of Oxford, United Kingdom
Vsevolod Samokhvalov, University of Liege, Belgium
Orest Semotiuk, Franko National University, Lviv
Viktoriya Sereda, NAS Institute of Ethnology, Lviv
Anton Shekhovtsov, University of Vienna, Austria
Andriy Shevchenko, Media Center Ukraine, Kyiv
Oxana Shevel, Tufts University, Medford, USA
Pavlo Shopin, National Pedagogical Dragomanov University, Kyiv
Karina Shyrokykh, Stockholm University, Sweden
Nadja Simon, freelance interpreter, Cologne, Germany
Olena Snigova, NAS Institute for Economics and Forecasting, Kyiv
Ilona Solohub, Analytical Platform "VoxUkraine," Kyiv
Iryna Solonenko, LibMod - Center for Liberal Modernity, Berlin
Galyna Solovei, National University of Kyiv-Mohyla Academy
Sergiy Stelmakh, NAS Institute of World History, Kyiv
Olena Stiazhkina, NAS Institute of the History of Ukraine, Kyiv
Dmitri Stratievski, Osteuropa Zentrum (OEZB), Berlin
Dmytro Stus, National Taras Shevchenko Museum, Kyiv
Frank Sysyn, University of Toronto, Canada
Olha Tokariuk, Center for European Policy Analysis, Washington
Olena Tregub, Independent Anti-Corruption Commission, Kyiv
Hlib Vyshlinsky, Centre for Economic Strategy, Kyiv
Mychailo Wynnyckyj, National University of Kyiv-Mohyla Academy
Yelyzaveta Yasko, NGO "Yellow Blue Strategy," Kyiv
Serhy Yekelchyk, University of Victoria, Canada
Victor Yushchenko, President of Ukraine 2005-2010, Kyiv
Oleksandr Zaitsev, Ukrainian Catholic University, Lviv
Kateryna Zarembo, National University of Kyiv-Mohyla Academy
Yaroslav Zhalilo, National Institute for Strategic Studies, Kyiv
Sergei Zhuk, Ball State University at Muncie, USA
Alina Zubkovych, Nordic Ukraine Forum, Stockholm
Liudmyla Zubrytska, National University of Kyiv-Mohyla Academy

Friends of the Series

Ana Maria Abulescu, University of Bucharest, Romania
Łukasz Adamski, Centrum Mieroszewskiego, Warsaw
Marieluise Beck, LibMod—Center for Liberal Modernity, Berlin
Marc Berensen, King's College London, United Kingdom
Johannes Bohnen, BOHNEN Public Affairs, Berlin
Karsten Brüggemann, University of Tallinn, Estonia
Ulf Brunnbauer, Leibniz Institute (IOS), Regensburg
Martin Dietze, German-Ukrainian Culture Society, Hamburg
Gergana Dimova, Florida State University, Tallahassee/London
Caroline von Gall, Goethe University, Frankfurt-Main
Zaur Gasimov, Rhenish Friedrich Wilhelm University, Bonn
Armand Gosu, University of Bucharest, Romania
Thomas Grant, University of Cambridge, United Kingdom
Gustav Gressel, European Council on Foreign Relations, Berlin
Rebecca Harms, European Centre for Press & Media Freedom, Leipzig
André Härtel, Stiftung Wissenschaft und Politik, Berlin/Brussels
Marcel Van Herpen, The Cicero Foundation, Maastricht
Richard Herzinger, freelance analyst, Berlin
Mieste Hotopp-Riecke, ICATAT, Magdeburg
Nico Lange, Munich Security Conference, Berlin
Martin Malek, freelance analyst, Vienna
Ingo Mannteufel, Broadcaster "Deutsche Welle," Bonn
Carlo Masala, Bundeswehr University, Munich
Wolfgang Mueller, University of Vienna, Austria
Dietmar Neutatz, Albert Ludwigs University, Freiburg
Torsten Oppelland, Friedrich Schiller University, Jena
Niccolò Pianciola, University of Padua, Italy
Gerald Praschl, German-Ukrainian Forum (DUF), Berlin
Felix Riefer, Think Tank Ideenagentur-Ost, Düsseldorf
Stefan Rohdewald, University of Leipzig, Germany
Sebastian Schäffer, Institute for the Danube Region (IDM), Vienna
Felix Schimansky-Geier, Friedrich Schiller University, Jena
Ulrich Schneckener, University of Osnabrück, Germany

Winfried Schneider-Deters, freelance analyst, Heidelberg/Kyiv
Gerhard Simon, University of Cologne, Germany
Kai Struve, Martin Luther University, Halle/Wittenberg
David Stulik, European Values Center for Security Policy, Prague
Andrzej Szeptycki, University of Warsaw, Poland
Philipp Ther, University of Vienna, Austria
Stefan Troebst, University of Leipzig, Germany

[Please send requests for changes in, corrections of, and additions to, this list to andreas.umland@stanforalumni.org.]

ibidem.eu

Zeitfracht Medien GmbH
Ferdinand-Jühlke-Straße 7
99095 Erfurt, Deutschland
produktsicherheit@kolibri360.de